THE LAW OF

GLOBAL COMMUNICATIONS

INTERNATIONAL LEGAL RESEARCH PROGRAM
COLUMBIA UNIVERSITY LAW SCHOOL PUBLICATIONS

Legal Aspects of Foreign Investment (W. Friedmann and R. C. Pugh, eds.), Little Brown & Co., 1959.

Joint International Business Ventures (W. Friedmann and G. Kalmanoff, eds.), Columbia University Press, 1961.

International Financial Aid (W. Friedmann, G. Kalmanoff, and R. F. Meagher), Columbia University Press, 1966.

Trade Agreements for Developing Countries (G. Verbit), Columbia University Press, 1969.

Government Enterprise (W. Friedmann and J. F. Garner, eds.), Stevens and Sons, Ltd., and Columbia University Press, 1970.

International Law and the Resources of the Sea (J. Andrassy), Columbia University Press, 1970.

Joint International Business Ventures in Developing Countries: Case Studies and Analysis of Recent Trends (W. Friedmann and Jean-Paul Béguin), Columbia University Press, 1971.

The Law of Global Communications (C. H. Alexandrowicz), Columbia University Press, 1971.

THE LAW
OF GLOBAL
COMMUNICATIONS

Charles Henry Alexandrowicz

COLUMBIA UNIVERSITY PRESS

NEW YORK and LONDON   1971

Charles Henry Alexandrowicz is a Fellow at the Centre of International Studies, Cambridge, England.

The preparation of this book was made possible by funds available to the International Legal Research Program from a grant made to Columbia University by the Ford Foundation.

TO MY WIFE

FOREWORD

Although the dangers to mankind's survival from the continuing absence of organized international security are becoming more evident every day, there is little prospect that institutionalized security against aggression will become a reality in the foreseeable future. National passions and conflicts appear to be stronger than ever. At best it may be hoped that a precarious balance of power and an instinct for self-preservation may prevent the numerous dangerous conflicts of our time from escalating into a third and final world war. On the other hand, there is an increasing realization that conditions of life on earth may become unbearable unless organized global cooperation in vital areas is greatly expanded, accelerated, and intensified. The three most urgent concerns appear to be the fields of conservation, development, and distribution of resources, protection of the environment, and communications. It is with the last of these, the field of global communications, that Professor Alexandrowicz's important study is concerned. It is in this area that, however hesitantly, the insight has come to the nations of the world that global communications' organizations, in the seas, in the air, and in outer space, are essential. To some extent at least, this transcends the ideological and political divisions of the world. Thus the Soviet Union —now a major factor in world air transport—a few months ago joined the International Civil Aviation Organization, while the danger of two rival systems persists in the field of international satellite communications. The need to create some order in the area of global communications also accounts for the remarkable extent to which certain decision-making powers have been openly or by acquiescence transferred from the member states to international organizations. In many cases, bilateral arrangements with nonmembers serve as substitutes for a truly global organization.

It would be impossible in this foreword to summarize the many developments traced in great detail by Professor Alexandrowicz in the areas of postal communications, radio transmissions, civil aviation, satellite communications, and maritime transport. The reason that the seas have, until recently, been virtually free of international regulation is, of course, the result of one of the most important accomplishments of the law of nations, the freedom of the seas. But modern technology and the intensification of maritime transport indicate the need to pass—in that as in other areas—from laissez faire to institutionalized regulation. The rapidly growing exploitation of the oceanbed resources, with all its attendant dangers of conflicting jurisdictions and the eventual partition of the oceans, makes the need for international organization even more urgent.[1]

The area of global communications may not be the most dramatic of the many urgent concerns in which mankind faces the alternative between chaos and organized cooperation. But it is one of the most important and perhaps more illuminating than any other area to demonstrate that necessity and common interests have produced certain progress, which may be summed up in three institutional developments: first, the gradual transfer, sometimes by acquiescence, of executive powers to the secretariats of international organizations, such as the Bureau of the UPU; second, the granting of certain quasi-legislative powers in some areas to certain international institutions, such as the ICAO and the WHO; third, the acknowledgment of the need for universal standards and organization by the assimilation of nonmember standards through bilateral arrangements. Sometimes—as recently in the case of the USSR's accession to the ICAO—full membership follows the interim arrangements.

---

[1] See, for a full discussion of these developments, Professor Juraj Andrassy's study, *International Law and the Resources of the Sea* (1970), which preceded Professor Alexandrowicz's monograph in the present series.

Much more remains to be done than has been accomplished. Nobody can regard the present structure of INTELSAT as satisfactory. And the functions and structure of IMCO are no more than a token of the overwhelming need to create effective international ocean regimes in the areas of navigation, fisheries, pollution, and development of mineral resources. But I am confident that Professor Alexandrowicz's study will prove to be an important contribution to the mechanisms of global cooperation in the growing number of fields where the need for institutionalized cooperation is rapidly becoming a matter not of ideology but of survival.

New York   WOLFGANG FRIEDMANN
March 1971

《《》》

ACKNOWLEDGMENTS

《《《》》

I wish to express my gratitude to all those who gave me guidance in the course of my research and assistance in the completion of this study.

My special thanks go to Professor Wolfgang Friedmann for the inspiration, encouragement, and advice he has given me throughout.

It was also my privilege to discuss problems relating to *The Law of Global Communications* with the legal or technical advisers of a number of Specialized Agencies of the United Nations. I would like to record my admiration for the work they carry out in the cause of international cooperation. The help they gave me was invaluable.

CONTENTS

THE LAW OF
GLOBAL COMMUNICATIONS

Ann. Fran. Droit Int'l   Annuaire Français de Droit International
Am. J. Int'l L.   American Journal of International Law
ANC   Air Navigation Commission (ICAO)
APT   automatic picture transmissions
ATC   Air Transport Committee (ICAO)
AT&T   American Telephone and Telegraph Company
Brit. Y. B. Int'l L.   British Year Book of International Law
CAB   Civil Aeronautics Board
CCIR   International Radio Consultative Committee (ITU)
CCITT   International Telegraph and Telephone Consultative
   Committee (ITU)
CCPS   Consultative Committee (Council) for Postal Studies (UPU)
CETS   European Conference on Satellite Telecommunications
CINA   Commission Internationale de Navigation Aérienne
COMSAT   Communications Satellite Corporation
EARC   Extraordinary Administrative Radio Conference-ITU
ECAC   European Civil Aviation Conference
FAO   Food and Agriculture Organization
FCC   Federal Communications Commission
GATT   General Agreement on Tariffs and Trade
HF   high-frequency
IATA   International Air Transport Association
IBRD   International Bank for Reconstruction and Development
ICAO   International Civil Aviation Organization
IFRB   International Frequency Registration Board
IMCO   Intergovernmental Maritime Consultative Organisation
IMF   International Monetary Fund
INTELSAT   International Telecommunications Satellite Consortium
ITU   International Telecommunication Union (International Telegraph
   Union)
MSC   Maritime Safety Committee (IMCO)
NASA   National Aeronautics and Space Administration
NTSB   National Transportation Safety Board (formerly CAB)
OAS   Organization of American States
PICAO   Provisional International Civil Aviation Organization
UNDP   United Nations Development Program
UNESCO   United Nations Educational Scientific and Cultural Organization
UPU   Universal Postal Union
WHO   World Health Organisation
WMO   World Meteorological Organisation
WWW   World Weather Watch

《《(O)》》》

INTRODUCTION

《《(O)》》》

The need for international communications is as old as the history of mankind. In conditions of modern technical progress it increasingly constitutes a global social reality. The law of global communication appears as the regulatory response to this need—a response in terms of rules of conduct which are meant to put the mechanism of world communication into proper shape. The international lawyer working on the rules of such a mechanism in the various fields of communication, shipping, civil aviation, telecommunication, and postal services is confronted with certain basic elements—namely, the physical context in which communication services are operable and actually operate, which may be called communication space, the vehicle or the means of communication which carry them out, and the persons, cargo, and messages which are the object of communication services. Each of these elements is governed by its own principles, but there is an intimate interconnection between them which contributes to various forms of organization and distribution of communication services in the international sphere.

This inquiry is made from the point of view of public international law and organization. The problems connected with this law arise out of the fact that vehicles of one nationality enter the territory of another sovereign on their international (global) routes or find themselves in an area of communication space outside sovereignty. If international communication services were carried out by a succession of vehicles (means of communication), each of which would perform only part of the serv-

ice within the area of its own nationality, few problems would arise.
This was the case with telegraphy before the establishment of the International Telegraph Union (ITU) in 1865. It is still the case with international postal services whenever the mail is transferred at frontier
points. But, generally speaking, international services carried out in this
way are complicated and, in any case, only possible on a regional
scale. Again, if vehicles of international communication were international, and not national in character, the problems connected with
traveling from one area of sovereignty to another would disappear. The
Constitution of the International Civil Aviation Organization (ICAO)
(Article 77) makes provision for aircraft operated by international
agencies, but the requirement of national registration of vehicles (aircraft) proved a difficult problem in the realization of the concept contained in Article 77.[1]

Thus, the major task of the student of the law of global communication is to examine the various ways and means by which it is possible
to organize global communication services by bridging the difference
between the nationality of the vehicle or means of communication (ship,
aircraft, satellite, frequency) and the nationality of the foreign space in
which the vehicle finds itself on its international route. Ships on international voyages sail on the high seas but enter the territorial waters and
harbors of another sovereign. Aircraft, leaving their national airports
and airspace, fly through foreign airspace or above the high seas to land
in foreign territories. Satellites, leaving their national launching sites,
move through the outer space, but they may return through the airspace
of another state or splash down into the high seas. Finally, radio waves,
transmitted by national stations at a given frequency, find themselves in
the electromagnetic radio space and are likely to be received in foreign
territory.

In all these cases the performance and coordination of services depends on the legal status of one or another communication space
through which a national vehicle travels on its international route. The
question of the legal status of communication space and its consequences therefore enjoy priority of discussion. Its definition in each case
is the concern of the international lawyer.

The more sovereignty has proved a disturbing factor in a particular branch of communication, the more difficult it has been to organize

global services on a multilateral and institutional level, as, for example, in civil aviation. On the other hand, in other branches of communication, global services, by overcoming the barriers of sovereignty, have reached a more or less centralized level of organization, sometimes combined with administrative machinery of coordination (for example, frequency regulation). Where the communication space has escaped fragmentation by sovereign interests, through the establishment of interest-sharing areas of international law (*res communis*), a better coordination and distribution of services could be contemplated or achieved (high seas, radio space, outer space).

While the legal status of operational communication space and the means of communication affect the organization and type of services, the running of services may dictate its own conditions and tend to affect the legal status of communication space. In international civil aviation the conditions of modern aircraft development make it increasingly difficult to conceive of sovereignty in airspace otherwise than on functional lines.

Whatever the situation with regard to the distribution (allocation) of services (whether it is carried out on the bilateral, multilateral, or institutional level), the means of communication (vehicles) which operate internationally must obey uniform technical rules of operation. This is particularly so in the field of civil aviation, in which commercial solutions are subordinated to a network of bilateral agreements. The highest degree of technical standardization is required to enable international carriers to operate their services in an efficient manner—hence, the establishment by ICAO of machinery for the promotion of uniform technical law.

The same applies to the fields of maritime transport and telecommunication and postal services. The relevant agencies, the Intergovernmental Maritime Consultative Organization (IMCO), the International Telecommunication Union (ITU), and the Universal Postal Union (UPU), have evolved their own machinery of technical lawmaking. Special attention will be drawn in this study to the development of regulatory and administrative techniques and quasi-legislative processes, and particularly to deviations from traditional treaty law in the practice of the agencies concerned with global communication.

These observations have, thus far, dealt with the first two elements of global communication, namely, operational communication space and the means (vehicle) of communication. A detailed discussion of the third element, persons, cargo, and messages, which are the objects of communication, is outside the scope of this inquiry. The legal status of passengers, crew, and cargo on board the vehicle on international routes is not the concern of public international law, within the framework of which this examination is carried out. Although the international lawyer is bound to deal with the problem of registration and nationality of the vehicle, and the ensuing introduction of a national law on board the vehicle, the details of this law belong to the field of municipal or comparative law. There are, however, certain treaty provisions transcending the field of public international law which deserve the attention of the student of international organization, since they deal with the question of legal order and avoidance of anarchy and lawlessness, for example, on board aircraft. It will therefore be necessary to make at least a few references to the relevant texts.

Finally, attention will be drawn to the international organs which are in charge of mechanisms of coordination or which are agencies for the promotion of uniform technical laws. A discussion of their structure will be undertaken, and the work methods of technical organs will be analyzed, particularly from the point of view of the development of a new technical and expert diplomacy. Discussion will not be extended to the details of the structure of the Specialized Agencies in the field of communication. Such discussion belongs to the general law of international organizations and need not be undertaken as it is not characteristic of the agencies in the field of communication. However, these agencies have created, in contrast to other organizations, certain technical organs and proceedings which constitute a specific feature of global communication and deserve special attention. Since they share certain types of procedures with the World Health Organisation (WHO) and the World Meteorological Organisation (WMO), some of the processes and practices of these two organizations will be examined comparatively with those of ICAO and IMCO. Moreover, the contribution of UPU, ITU, and ICAO to the development of institutionalized arbitral procedures will be examined.

The discussion of public organs of global communication will be extended to an examination of certain mixed (public and private) agencies which perform quasi-public functions and supplement the work of intergovernmental agencies or carry out tasks which the latter are unable to perform. The International Air Transport Association (IATA) and the International Telecommunications Satellite Consortium (INTELSAT) are organizations of this type.

In the general conclusions a comparative survey of some of the features which all agencies of global communication have in common will be attempted. Such a survey presents some difficulties in view of the fact that the four branches of communication, despite the similarities between them, do not lend themselves in all respects to a comparative inquiry. The agencies which institutionalized them had appeared in two separate groups: first, ITU and UPU, which developed on parallel lines since the early second half of the nineteenth century; and later, in different circumstances, the agencies dealing with international civil aviation and shipping. But whatever the initial differences between these agencies, they have established, in the course of time, a type of regime with similar expert organs and procedures of technical lawmaking. Some of the institutions which emerged out of this process of lawmaking constitute a significant contribution to the development of the contemporary international law of cooperation.[2]

THE LEGAL STATUS OF THE OPERATIONAL COMMUNICATION SPACE AND ITS IMPACT ON THE ORGANIZATION OF GLOBAL SERVICES

《《（O）》》》》》》》》》》》》》》》》》》》》》》》》》》》》》》》》》》》

MARITIME TRANSPORT

Discussion of the operational space of global communication will open here with an examination of the position of oceanic routes in the classical law of nations. Shipping is the most ancient branch of world communication, and already the seventeenth century witnessed an intensive interest of international lawyers in defining the legal status of the high seas. This came in reaction to the great discoveries which opened unprecedented possibilities of trade between Europe and other continents. The issue of *mare liberum* versus *mare clausum* resulted in the general acceptance of the principle of the freedom of the sea in international customary law. It is possible that Grotius, its main promoter, conceived of it under the influence of problems which arose out of the activities of the Dutch East India Company in the East. When Grotius, as counsel of the company, was called upon to pronounce himself on the capture of a Portuguese vessel by the Dutch in the straits of Malacca, he studied the facts of the case in the archives of the company before writing his *De*

Jure Praedae. Chapter XII of this work, dealing with the freedom of the sea, was published in 1608. Grotius learned from his preliminary studies that while according to state practice in Europe the great maritime powers (Venice, Genoa, Portugal, Spain, and England) claimed sovereignty over far-reaching parts of the high seas, the East Indian maritime powers followed a customary regime of the freedom of the sea. This concept found expression in, *inter alia,* the thirteenth-century maritime codes of Macassar and Malacca (translated into French and published by Pardessus in 1845). There is good reason to believe that when Grotius advocated, on behalf of the Dutch, the principle of the freedom of the sea in opposition to Spanish and Portuguese claims to sovereignty over oceanic routes, he found support for his arguments in ancient maritime practice in the East.[1]

Grotius's initiative cast doubt on claims to sovereignty over the routes of global communication which are essential to world trade. Trade and communications were obstructed by claims of a monopolistic character raised by some of the maritime powers in the sixteenth century and earlier.

The principle of the freedom of the sea, which became part and parcel of international customary law, is embodied in the Geneva Convention on the High Sea (1958). If Grotius were to write his *Mare Liberum* today, he would not, under present circumstances, be able to use the argument of impossibility of physical control of the high sea by states; but he would still be able to rely on the social reality of world intercourse and the reciprocal interest of the member states of the family of nations to abide by the freedom of the sea. In fact, in spite of technical developments which open up the possibility of far-reaching control over oceanic routes, the principle has not so far been dislodged for fear of breakdown of a maritime regime which states cannot afford to abandon.

One of the most remarkable consequences of the freedom of the sea and the absence of national sovereignty has been the concomitant absence of any need of arrangements between states. The noninterference of states in the past allowed private initiative to organize shipping on a worldwide scale extending to a wide range of services, first cargo and then passenger. But there are a number of factors which counteract the beneficial impact of the legal status of the sea on the organization of maritime services. In order to understand the effect and influence of these factors a few preliminary observations may be offered.

Although the legal status of the high sea is a factor promoting the development and growth of maritime services on a multilateral scale, mainly in the private sector, the question of access of ships to foreign harbors has not been solved satisfactorily in either international customary law or by treaties. Grotius called for the right of free access of vessels to foreign harbors as essential for purposes of world trade. A number of writers tried to uphold the right to free access but state practice does not seem to support such a right at present.

It will be recalled that the arbitral tribunal in the dispute between the government of Saudi Arabia and the Arabian American Oil Company declared itself in favor of the existence of a right of free access.[2] It stated that "the ports of every State must be open to foreign merchant vessels and can only be closed when the vital interests of the State so require." This, the tribunal said, is a principle of public international law which finds support in Article 16 of the statute on the international regime of maritime ports, established by the Geneva Conference of 1923. The right of access of vessels to foreign harbors would therefore imply the right to carry out the international services in which a vessel is engaged, namely, to load and unload cargo or embark and disembark passengers. The tribunal also referred to the Geneva Convention on the Regime of Maritime Ports of 1923, which provides for equality of treatment of foreign vessels with national vessels as far as access to harbors is concerned.[3] However, the provisions of this convention are not necessarily *declaratory* of international customary law.[4] Moreover, the convention, although it constituted an attempt to bring about the solution of a pressing problem on the multilateral level, was far from universal. Some of the leading maritime powers, such as the United States and the Soviet Union, did not ratify it.

In view of this it is not possible to assume that access to foreign harbors is more than a usage in international law. There is no generally accepted *opinio juris* which could have converted the usage into a right of access. Thus, the basic impact of the legal status of the sea on the operation of global maritime services is to some extent reduced by the situation in which vessels find themselves upon entering foreign harbors. The absence of a right to enter foreign inland waters underlines the sovereign prerogative granted by international customary law with regard to the admission or nonadmission of ships to territorial waters, except perhaps for ships in distress.

Since the Geneva Convention of 1923 is not an effective multilateral remedy to the restrictions resulting from sovereignty, the only solution left open to states has been to conclude bilateral treaties. Indeed, today a network of such treaties provides a legally more reliable answer than the usage of free access. The situation of maritime transport is thus similar to that of air transport, where bilateralism of transport services reigns supreme. But there are other factors which have been instrumental in the growth of bilateralism in maritime transport and deserve further attention. In order to understand the operation of these factors the following observations on the organization of maritime services may be offered.[5]

Maritime services performed by merchant vessels can be classified into services by ships carrying specific bulk cargos, such as wheat and oil, and ships carrying general cargo, a heterogeneous range of commodities and manufactured goods. The first type of cargo is usually carried at low rates in ships hired for a particular voyage (tramps) and is not part of regular (scheduled) shipping services. On the other hand, general cargo tends to be carried on cargo liners running on specific routes and requiring regularity of services and stability of rates. The situation is *mutatis mutandis* similar to that of scheduled and nonscheduled air services.

The nineteenth century witnessed extensive and unregulated competition in the field of shipping, and shipowners, in order to counteract its adverse effects, formed associations or conferences for coordinating and defending their interests.[6] The first conference of this kind was formed in 1892 to cover the oceanic route between Europe and India; other conferences followed later. A conference is a private international association of shipping lines, and it may be either an informal body or an organization in the strict sense of the word with a permanent secretariat. It aims at restricting competition, fixing freights, and planning schedules to be observed by liners on international routes. The significant advantage of conferences is the existence of a rate-fixing machinery outside the sphere of government action. Because under this system governments are not directly involved in rate conflicts, there is in principle less international friction and dissent. In the long run, however, governments cannot be indifferent to the regulatory activities of their shipping lines (often of a quasi-public character) which affect their relations with other countries. Intervention by governments tends to follow such awareness.

Government intervention has occurred in many countries through subsidies, flag discrimination, or other forms of restrictions aiming at support for national shipping interests. The more such intervention in various countries has interfered with the maintenance and progress of international services in one way or another, the more necessary it has been to seek solutions on the intergovernmental level. The tendency has been to resort to bilateral interstate arrangements. All these developments tend to reduce the original beneficial impact of the freedom of the seas upon the running of shipping services.

After the establishment of IMCO in 1958 the question arose whether the machinery available through the new organization could contribute to the solution of international problems.[7] The IMCO Convention divides the purposes of the organization into those relating to technical matters and those relating to economic affairs (Article 1). As to the latter, IMCO is authorized "to encourage the removal of discriminatory action and unnecessary restrictions by governments affecting shipping engaged in international trade."

Thus, IMCO can in principle act in the area of flag discrimination, a restrictive element in world trade. IMCO may also deal with "unfair restrictive practices by shipping concerns" (Article 1); Article 4 lays down the conditions of such IMCO intervention. But in practice IMCO has never resorted to the exercise of its jurisdiction in economic matters. It has not been forgotten that the ratification of its convention was delayed for ten years because of fear of IMCO interference in matters which national shipping concerns or authorities consider their exclusive sphere and which may lead to acute interstate conflicts.[8] Thus IMCO concentrates entirely on regulation of technical matters and abstains from the solution of questions relating to the distribution and allocation of world services, rates to be fixed for these services, and other commercial matters.[9]

In these circumstances bilateralism is as prominent in maritime transport as in the field of scheduled air transport, which does not enjoy the advantage of an open world airspace. If these fields of global communication are compared, a striking feature is the difference in the legal status of the operational communication space with different results for the organization of services and with trends in opposite directions. While maritime transport tends to lose some of the advantages which it drew for centuries from the legal status of the sea [10] and while state intervention leads to bilateral solutions which are restrictive in their effect, air transport, in spite of the disadvantages resulting from the legal status of the airspace (sovereignty) and in spite of being confined to a network of bilateral transport agreements, has tended to free itself from the latter and to modify the concept of sovereignty in the airspace.

CIVIL AVIATION

The firm establishment of the concept of sovereignty with regard to the airspace was preceded by controversies over its legal status in international law before World War I. Professor Paul Fauchille (*Le Grotius aérien*) advocated free airspace open to all nations of the world, subject only to the right of each state to security and self-defense. The Institute of International Law gave its support to this idea in 1906, but it had no chance of taking root in state practice. In 1910 an international conference on air navigation met in Paris, providing the first significant forum for an exchange of views between states. The records of the conference show that the nineteen participating states claimed sovereignty in the airspace above their territory, but the claim was not generally one for unrestricted sovereignty. Some delegates advocated the principle of the freedom of passage of foreign aircraft and they relied on a possible analogy between air law and maritime law, particularly on the usage of access of vessels to foreign harbors and to nondiscriminatory treatment of ships in such harbors and territorial waters.

The Paris Conference of 1910 failed to establish an international organization but the rapid development of aircraft during World War I and the prospects of an expanding commercial air industry made the foundation of such an organization inevitable after the end of the war. In 1919 a number of powers signed a convention creating the International Commission for Air Navigation (Commission Internationale de Navigation Aérienne—CINA).

In the next twelve years ratification of, or instruments of adherence to the above convention, called the Paris Convention, were deposited in Paris by sixteen European powers including Great Britain and France (but excluding Germany and the Soviet Union) and by twelve non-European powers (excluding the United States).[11] CINA never became a global organization although it established cooperation in the West European region with important extensions to Central and Eastern Europe, and to the dominions as well as to the colonies of contracting states. Despite its less than global character, the achievements of CINA as a pioneering agency are of considerable significance. We shall discuss later the new legislative procedures which it established for passing technical air law (Annexes). What is important for purposes of the present discussion is the definition which it adopted for the legal status of airspace.

Article 1 of the convention defined, for the first time in the history of aerial navigation, the position of airspace in international law. It stated that "the High Contracting Parties recognise that every power has *complete and exclusive* [12] sovereignty over the air space above its territory." While the British delegation at the Paris Conference insisted on the formula of "complete and exclusive" sovereignty in the air, it also advocated a limitation on sovereignty by the introduction of the principle of freedom of innocent passage. The other participating powers agreed to this principle but they wished to exclude from its benefit the former enemy states. Thus sovereignty in the air was envisaged as "complete and exclusive" in relation to these states only. Prima facie it seemed to remain a concept of limited validity in relation to the majority of powers. Article 2 adopted the principle of freedom of passage in the following words: "Each contracting State undertakes in time of peace to accord freedom of innocent passage above its territory to the aircraft of the other contracting States, provided that the conditions laid down in the present convention are observed." [13] According to Article 15 "every aircraft of a contracting State has the right to cross the airspace of another State without landing." [14] However, the further text of the article referring to conditions of landing of foreign aircraft stipulates in the last paragraph that "the establishment of international airways shall be subject to the consent of the States flown over." A later protocol of amendment of Article 15 required prior authorization for the establishment of international airways as well as for the creation and operation of regular international air navigation lines with or without landing in foreign territory.[15]

The above provisions proved decisive for the development of international civil aviation. Whatever the original intentions of the contracting parties may have been as to the significance of "complete and exclusive" sovereignty in airspace, the ultimate meaning of this definition as adopted by the vast majority of states proved to be highly restrictive for international civil aviation.

At the International Air Conference in 1929 the principle of freedom of traffic was conclusively abandoned. Considerations of security and increasing fear of commercial competition prevailed over the earlier liberal views. The amendment of Article 15 made it quite clear that scheduled (regular) international air services would depend upon bilateral agreements between pairs of countries or upon unilateral permission of entry. If the operation of scheduled air services in the airspace or territory of a foreign country required prior authorization by the latter, it was obvious that states would insist on exchanging concessions with other states through bargaining within bilateral channels rather than within a multilateral framework.

The problems which had been considered by the founders of CINA in 1919 were reconsidered by the states participating in the Chicago Conference of 1944. Before discussing the ultimate approach of the conference to the definition of the legal status of the airspace which was to find its place in the Chicago Convention of 1944, some of its background should be recalled.

The Chicago Conference was faced with a number of proposals relating to the establishment of the new civil aviation agency and to the settlement of fundamental problems of air navigation and air services. Among the proposals, those submitted by the United States, the United Kingdom, Canada, and Australia-New Zealand should be mentioned. While the United States wished the new agency to be confined to the regulation of technical matters, the United Kingdom plan proposed the extension of its jurisdiction to the regulation of commercial aspects of civil aviation. Under this proposal the new agency would have *inter alia*

14 LEGAL STATUS OF COMMUNICATION SPACE

fixed rates for carriage by air. The Canadian plan went further and proposed the establishment of a regulatory agency on the pattern of the Civil Aeronautics Board (CAB) in the United States. It would have issued certificates to airlines granting them the right to operate services over certain international routes. Finally, the proposal of the Australian and New Zealand governments suggested the creation of a world air corporation which would own and operate aircraft on international routes. All these proposals (except that submitted by the United States) had little chance of general acceptance. The powers were far from ready to adopt any plan for a multilateral and institutionalized regime of air services.

The Chicago Conference(s) reached a precarious compromise solution by adopting three major agreements: 1) The Convention on International Civil Aviation, which established ICAO and regulated mainly technical matters; [16] 2) the International Air Transport Agreement; and 3) the International Air Service Transit Agreement. The first agreement defines the legal status of airspace in Article 1, which adopts the same formula as that followed by the Paris Convention of 1919. According to this article "the contracting States recognise that every State [17] has complete and exclusive sovereignty over the airspace above its territory." [18] Attention has been drawn to the impact of this formula on the organization of international scheduled air services from the commercial point of view. Under the CINA regime, the establishment of international airways had been subject to the consent of states flown over, and of States receiving foreign aircraft. Prior authorization for the creation of scheduled international airlines was required. Under Article 6 of the ICAO Convention "no scheduled international air service may be operated over or into the territory of a contracting State except with the special permission or other authorisation of that State and in accordance with the terms of such permission or authorisation." It was quite obvious that this provision meant the perpetuation of the regime of bilateralism for international scheduled services. However, Article 5 adopts a more progressive solution.[19] The first part of this article relates to nonscheduled flights and here the contracting grantee state receives the benefit of the first and second freedoms of the air. The second part of the article relates to nonscheduled flights, particularly of a commercial character, permitting the grantee state to take on or to discharge passengers, mail, and cargo.[20] The grantor state may, however, impose conditions on this right which would include prior authorization. Such authorization is in principle not required for nonscheduled flights of a noncommercial character as stated in part one of Article 5.

The first and second freedoms of the air have been extended to scheduled flights by the International Air Service Transit Agreement, also called the Two Freedom Agreement. This agreement was concluded in Chicago but it remained outside the main convention establishing ICAO. It allows aircraft on international scheduled flights to fly across the territory of the other contracting states and to land in their territory for nontraffic purposes such as refueling or carrying out repairs. This agreement proved successful and it is adhered to by most of the powers. It does not directly affect their commercial interests in the field of international civil aviation.

At the Chicago Conference, the United States sponsored the conclusion of a further agreement, namely, the International Air Transport Agreement, which, apart from the first two freedoms, also grants three commercial freedoms to the contracting states. These consist of the privilege to discharge passengers, mail, and cargo taken on in the territory of the state whose nationality the aircraft possesses; the privilege to take on passengers, mail, and cargo for the territory of such a state; and the privilege to take on passengers, mail, and cargo for the territory of any contracting state and to discharge passengers, mail, and cargo arriving from any contracting state.[21]

In this agreement traffic rights relate only to through services on a route constituting a reasonably direct line out from and back to the homeland of the state whose nationality the aircraft possesses. The agreement attempted more than most of the powers were ready to concede in the field of international air commerce, and it was ratified by only a few countries. Actually, civil aviation has tended to remain an instrument of national policy and an immediate multilateral solution on a global commercial scale still seems premature. Scheduled international services have been and are left to bilateral agreements between states. But bilateralism is far from static in this field, since the law has to respond to the rapid development of air navigation and air transport. Although the change from bilateral to multilateral solutions is much slower than in other fields of communication—such as in postal and tele-

communication services where the establishment of UPU and ITU sub-
stituted global regulation for bilateral relations—it is nevertheless im-
perceptibly in progress. Several factors tend to contribute to such
progress.

These factors can be divided into those which have appeared
within the existing system of air services and those which have appeared outside this system. An important factor in the first category is
the establishment of standard forms of the typical bilateral transport
agreement which has contributed, to some extent, to uniformity of bilateral relations.

The first standard form of bilateral agreement for the exchange of
commercial rights relating to scheduled air services is to be found in the
final act of the Chicago Conference of 1944. In 1959 the European
Civil Aviation Conference (ECAC) produced a new set of standard
clauses for bilateral agreements (on a regional scale), which to some extent follow the Chicago pattern.[22] The Secretariat of ICAO carried out
a comparative study of administrative clauses and prepared a *Handbook
on Administrative Clauses in Bilateral Air Transport Agreements*.[23]
This publication shows a measure of uniformity of standard provisions
subject to certain differences between states. Each section of the handbook consists of three parts: the Chicago form standard clauses, the
ECAC standard clauses, and a summary of views of member states on
the above clauses. The last part makes frequent reference to the Bermuda Agreement, the bilateral air transport arrangement entered into
by the United States and the United Kingdom in 1946, which is of particular interest as a model agreement. It constitutes a compromise between the competitive approach to scheduled services as advocated by
the United States and the United Kingdom approach which tends to impose restrictions on the freedom of running air services.

Among the problems which require a solution within the framework of the bilateral agreement, the most significant one deals with the
division of traffic between the contracting states.[24] Two solutions are
possible: one by a predetermined arrangement of traffic-sharing, which
leaves nothing to competition or chance; the other by allowing competition, though subject to formulae which keep it under control. If the
predetermination method is adopted the parties set, in advance, the actual division of traffic capacity,[25] and they cannot exceed their shares.

This formula was applied prior to Bermuda but it also exists in some of the post-Bermuda agreements such as in the United States–India Agreement of 1956. Such a fixed division of traffic is *mutatis mutandis* comparable to flag discrimination in shipping, but the term is not used in civil aviation.[26]

The Bermuda Agreement introduced a new formula in place of the determination clause. This formula consists of the fair and equal opportunity clause combined with the use of national traffic as primary capacity justification subject to *ex post facto* review.[27] Its component elements deserve a more detailed examination. The Bermuda Conference resolved "that the two contracting Governments desire to foster and encourage the widest possible distribution of benefits of air travel for the general good of mankind at the cheapest rate consistent with sound economic principles. . . ." [28]

While the concept of predetermination and *a priori* division of traffic tends to be restrictive by its very nature,[29] the Bermuda Agreement combines the cooperative approach with flexible expansionist solutions. It does not define the meaning of "fair and equal opportunity," but it is understood that in the operation of the airlines of one contracting party the interests of airlines of the other party will be taken into account. The services provided by a designated airline retain as their primary objective the provision of capacity adequate to traffic demands between the country of which such airline is a national (home country) and the country of ultimate destination of the traffic. Thus the primary objective of each airline is its own third- and fourth- freedom traffic. On the other hand, the right to embark and disembark international traffic destined for or coming from third countries, at points stipulated in the Annex to the Bermuda Agreement (fifth-freedom traffic), is exercised in such a way as to relate capacity: (1) to the traffic requirements between the country of origin and the country of destination; (2) to the requirements of through airline operations;[30] and (3) to the traffic requirements of the area through which the airline passes after taking account of local and regional services.[31]

The superiority of this system over the predetermination regime lies in the fact that rigid market-sharing is avoided as detrimental to a competitive expansion of services. The Bermuda Agreement restricts competition in third- and fourth-freedom traffic only, allowing each airline to carry its national share (primary justification) but it admits fifth-freedom traffic on a fill-up basis (secondary justification). The ratio of secondary to primary justification traffic is reviewed *ex post facto* with the help of statistics and if the former exceeds the latter steps would be taken to adjust the position.[32]

The term "national" traffic calls for explanation. The Bermuda Agreement refers in this respect to the nationality of the airline and to the exercise by such airline of third- and fourth-freedom traffic, namely, the particular state's own traffic.[33] If the above use of the term "national" is compared with its use in the Air Transport Agreement of 1944, it will be seen that the latter refers to the nationality of the aircraft and not of airlines. This may be misleading, for both agreements, in spite of the differences between them, have as their objective the sharing of traffic in a bilateral or multilateral way. But in the multilateral agreement [34] nationality of the airline seems to be irrelevant in the definition of freedoms 3 and 4 (the position is the same in the Transit Agreement), while in the bilateral agreement the nationality of aircraft is ignored. However, what matters in the distribution of traffic is the character of the airline, irrespective of whether it uses aircraft of its own nationality or foreign aircraft. The same conclusion emerges from Article 6 of the Chicago Convention, which states that no scheduled international air service may be operated over or into the territory of a contracting state without the latter's permission. While in this article the prohibition is addressed to an "air service," freedoms 1 and 2, in respect of nonscheduled services, are granted in Article 5 to aircraft of the state concerned.[35] There is perhaps room for some adjustment of terminology to the ultimate intentions of the contracting parties in the various agreements.

It follows from these observations that the uniformity of the model bilateral agreement, particularly of the Bermuda type, has tended to standardize the network of bilateral arrangements and created a sort of cryptomultilateral regime and thus counteracted the adverse effects of "complete and exclusive" sovereignty in airspace, with its restrictive consequences for scheduled air services.

Among other counteracting factors within the existing system of air services is the incompatibility of methods of modern air traffic control with the division of world airspace by political frontiers. To understand the details of this problem, a brief discussion of the provisions of Annex 11 of the Chicago Convention is necessary.

Chapter 2 of the Annex states that the "contracting States shall determine in accordance with the provisions of this Annex and for the territories over which they have jurisdiction these portions of the airspace . . . where air traffic services will be provided. . . . They shall thereafter establish and supervise such services." But delegation of power is permitted in those cases in which jurisdictional areas of air traffic services do not coincide with areas of sovereignty, in other words when it is physically or functionally impossible to run air traffic services in portions of the airspace determined by political frontiers. As will be shown, this is not infrequently the case.

The objectives of air traffic services are: (1) to prevent collisions between aircraft; (2) to prevent collisions between aircraft on the maneuvering area and obstructions in that area; (3) to expedite and maintain an orderly flow of air traffic; (4) to provide advice and information useful for the safe and efficient conduct of flights; (5) to notify appropriate organizations regarding aircraft in need of search and rescue and to assist such organizations as required. Air traffic services can be divided into air traffic control services, flight information services, and alerting services.[36] A flight information region is a portion of the airspace where it is determined that a flight information service and alerting service will be provided.[37] The Annex defines control areas and control zones as portions of the airspace where an air traffic control service is provided.[38]

In normal circumstances each country runs its own air traffic control services within the limits of its airspace.[39] Thus, whenever aircraft on international flights cross the boundaries of a national airspace, they fly from one jurisdiction into another. It follows from the above that there must be suitably located transfer points, mutually agreed by the contracting parties. When the aircraft passes from one block of national airspace into another area of sovereignty, the responsibility for control of such aircraft must be transferred from one control unit to another, according to established rules.[40] Aircraft control units have the power to authorize an aircraft to proceed on its route (air traffic control clearance) and various units coordinate their clearance to cover the entire route of an aircraft.[41] Units advise each other about the flight of aircraft in order to control air traffic flow.[42] The other chapters of Annex 11 deal with the flight information service (Chapter 4),[43] the alerting service (Chapter 5),[44] air traffic service requirements (Chapter 6),[45] and meteorological information (Chapter 7).

The question may arise whether delegation of air traffic control jurisdiction by one state to another is a matter of discretion to be exercised by the delegating state, as it would be under the rules of international law, or whether such delegation may also be the compelling consequence of air traffic requirements, particularly connected with the rapidly progressing flow of international air traffic. Certain national reports relating to questions connected with air traffic control and submitted to the Legal Committee of ICAO deserve attention.[46] Although they deal primarily with liability of air traffic control agencies, they also reflect the challenge of a rapidly developing world air traffic and the need of regulatory measures to deal with urgent problems.

A Swiss report refers to airspace reduction, which is due not only to increased flight speeds but also to the increasing number of aircraft in operation. It must be apportioned and organized to ensure its optimum utilization, which can only be done by means of positive control of air traffic. The report further states that the vertical division of the airspace may cause considerable difficulties, particularly because of military aviation. According to a Swedish report, "the expected increase in traffic will attain such proportions by the end of the century that, if the same degree of safety is maintained, the average incidence of accidents will reach one serious accident per day. . . ." [47] High flight speed requires very extensive zones which cannot be limited to national boundaries; in certain areas this leads almost directly to the establishment of international coordination by the creation of international air traffic control services, such as Eurocontrol and the Corporacion Centroamericana de Servicios de Navegacion Aerea.

Eurocontrol made an agreement with the Federal Aviation Agency of the United States for the control of international air movements and, as a result, many states redesigned their controlled airspace, including delineation of new airways and control areas within which modern automatic processes are applied.[48] Moreover, civil aviation and shipping require a substantially improved system of coordinated traffic control covering both fields of communication. Coordination services are expected to receive periodic position reports from aircraft and ships under their cognizance. More frequent position reports would increase safety. Satellites could meet the demand better than conventional means of reporting. Ground stations would be able to pool a rich volume of information which would be available to various agencies, particularly those concerned with search and rescue activities. This system would also be helpful for more efficient routing of aircraft and ships to avoid adverse weather conditions. The navigators concerned would receive accurate information on a global scale through satellites.[49]

These comments concerning recent developments in the field of communication point to the need for improved navigational guidance. In the field of civil aviation, flight characteristics of aircraft have an impact on the airspace system, and it is obviously necessary to keep its structure relatively simple and manageable. Blocks of airspace where traffic services are provided should be so delineated (in both the vertical and horizontal dimensions) "as to minimize the number of transfers of control jurisdiction" that is, the change from one air traffic control unit to another, which aircraft on international routes must respect.[50] The air traffic control situation is different in various parts of the world. From the point of view of geographical configuration, difficulties arise with delineation of airspace in vast regions in which political frontiers are not ascertainable with precision, such as in Africa or in parts of Asia. Geographical aspects must be considered jointly with the density of traffic and with recent political changes in the two continents. In former colonial territories the delineation of air traffic control units often deviated from political frontiers which were agreed between the metropolitan powers. The independent African states insist on strict respect for political boundaries and the corresponding portions of the airspace.[51] Moreover, the density of traffic in these areas is comparatively low, and thus conditions under which transnational air traffic control units would deviate from political frontiers rarely arise.

The same would apply to low density traffic areas in parts of East Europe, the Middle East, and South America. In other areas, however, traffic congestion, the use of modern aircraft, high altitude flying, and other circumstances automatically tend to reduce the significance of the division of airspace according to political frontiers. It has already been noted that Eurocontrol was established to pool traffic control services in

Europe. A similar arrangement exists for the Central American Flight Information Region.

The ICAO Council showed considerable foresight when it adopted the following significant recommendation in Chapter 2 of Annex 11: [52] "The delineation of airspace wherein air traffic services are to be provided should be related to the nature of the route structure and the need for efficient service rather than to national boundaries." Note 1 to this rule consequently recommends the conclusion of agreements to permit the delineation of airspace lying across national boundaries whenever such action facilitates the providing of air traffic services.[53] Note 2 refers to delegation of responsibility for air traffic control by one state to another and states that such delegation is not in "derogation of its national sovereignty." In practice, however, delegation or transfer of air traffic control powers across national boundaries is often carried out on the level of informal arrangements between civil aviation authorities and not by formal intergovernmental agreement.[54] Thus arrangements have been made between the Flight Information Regions in Geneva and Zurich and civil aviation units in France and Germany. This development must be considered jointly with other possible limitations to the concept of national sovereignty in airspace, both vertically and horizontally (outer space). The rapid expansion of world civil aviation is bound to give new significance to national sovereignty in airspace which cannot be conceived as a complete and exclusive right of the subjacent sovereign (Article 1 of the Chicago Convention) but is circumscribed by his duty to exercise certain responsibilities of a *functional* nature. These responsibilities are connected with the existence of a global network which does not lend itself entirely to divisions according to political frontiers but calls for delineation primarily "related to the nature of route structure(s) and need for efficient service" (see Annex 11:2,7).

The element of functionalism which emerges from the provisions of Annex 11 of the Chicago Convention can also be found in Annexes 12 and 13. Annex 12 contains the rules relating to the operation of search and rescue services in the territories of the contracting states and over the neighboring seas, and to coordination of such services with those of neighboring states. Annex 13 is concerned with aircraft accident inquiries and contains the details of an administrative procedure of inquiry indicating the lessons which can be learned from such inquiries for the improvement of safety of aircraft flight. The entity designated to conduct the inquiry is the state in which the accident occurs (Inquiry State). But according to Article 26 of the Chicago Convention, the state in which the aircraft is registered "shall be given the opportunity to appoint observers to be present at the inquiry and the State holding the inquiry shall communicate the report and findings in the matter to that State."

Annexes 12 and 13 should be treated jointly with Annex 11 because of the impact of present-day developments in international civil aviation on national sovereignty. Just as modern air traffic control frequently ignores national frontiers, search, rescue and accident inquiry require the establishment of areas and procedures which are transsovereign in character. Thus Chapter 3 of Annex 12, referring to search and rescue areas, provides that "those (areas) may extend beyond national boundaries." Moreover, the elaborate procedure of accident investigation, which is in the nature of a quasi-judicial inquiry, constitutes a framework in which all states concerned cooperate, irrespective of their national interests.

Another factor reducing the value of the present regime of scheduled air services results from the impossibility of establishing a precise distinction between scheduled and nonscheduled air services. The difference between the two has far-reaching consequences, for Article 6 of the Chicago Convention states that "no scheduled international air service may be operated over or into the territory of a contracting State except with the special permission or other authorisation of that State. . . ."

On the other hand, according to Article 5 of the convention, aircraft of one contracting sovereign which are on nonscheduled flights have the right to pass in transit nonstop over the territory of another contracting sovereign or to stop for nontraffic purposes. If such aircraft carry passengers, cargo, or mail for remuneration or hire, they have the "privilege" (the word "right" is not used here) of taking on or discharging passengers, cargo, or mail, subject to the right of the sovereign (affected by such commercial activity) to impose regulations, conditions, or limitations on foreign aircraft. Thus the distinction between scheduled and nonscheduled flights is significant, and the Chicago Convention might have been expected to include a definition of scheduled service in the text.[55] In the absence of such a definition in the convention, we must look elsewhere for guidance. The ICAO Council has indicated three essential conditions which are characteristic of a scheduled flight: (1) There must be a systematic series of flights between two or more different countries; (2) the air service must be carried out for remuneration; (3) a timetable must be offered to the public, and services must be carried out irrespective of whether payload is available (7278, C 841, 10/5 1952).

Difficulties can arise in the practical application of this definition. Certain flights are outside the category of scheduled services, such as services carried out on behalf of specific groups of passengers, namely, emigrants or pilgrims or teams of sportsmen or other persons. In the absence of a precise definition in the convention, it is often difficult to classify a particular flight as scheduled or nonscheduled. If a chartered flight, which is intended to be nonscheduled and operates a commercial service, offers some seats to the general public (if only on a fill-up basis), it tends to become a cryptoscheduled flight. It would then, according to Article 6 of the Chicago Convention, be subject to the requirement of special authorization by the foreign sovereign into whose territory or airspace it enters. Yet, in fact, it operates as a nonscheduled flight and takes advantage of Article 5, which does not require special permission or other authorization, though the receiving sovereign may impose on nonscheduled commercial flights coming from abroad its regulations, conditions, or limitations. The existence of these cryptoscheduled flights is no doubt a further factor cutting into the present regime of air transport as based on "complete and exclusive" sovereignty over the airspace.

Some of the factors counteracting the present-day system of air services (based on sovereignty and bilateralism) from within the system have been discussed. There is also an important external factor operating in the same direction, namely, outer space communication. Outer space activities have brought about a response of the law in the sense of discarding notions of national sovereignty in the exoatmospheric region (see Outer Space Treaty of 1966, Chapter 1, note 75). Satellites move in a global communication space which does not lend itself to national appropriation. In fact, it is possible to conceive it as *res communis,* that is, as an area of shared interests, a concept which had earlier become the basis for the regime of the high sea and for radiocommunication.

The question has been frequently asked whether the frontier between airspace and outer space is physically ascertainable. This question cannot be answered in terms of a precise boundary line. Generally it can be said that airspace ends where the aerodynamic lift ceases to operate and outer space begins where orbital forces take over.

ICAO is already concerned with airspace aspects of satellite communication such as the passing of satellites through the airspace of a foreign country, particularly on their way back to earth. The concept of national sovereignty in the space above the territory of a state *usque ad coelum* can no longer be upheld.[56]

The possible demarcation line between airspace and outer space was discussed at the fifty-second Conference of the International Law Association in 1966.[57] It was felt that certain rules based on recent state practice could be suggested. Specifically, no state has ever complained about violation of sovereignty in connection with the hundreds of satellites which are or have been orbiting the earth. The firm conviction was expressed that airspace cannot reach beyond the lowest perigee of any satellite placed in orbit so far. It may be noted that the lowest perigee is about eighty miles above earth, or thirty miles further out than the proposed von Karman line. In fact there is no generally accepted fixed boundary line, just as there is no fixed international rule regarding the outer limit of territorial waters. Whatever the situation, no state can claim sovereignty within the area of operation of orbital forces which indicate the limit to geocentric law.

Outer space developments are bound to have an impact on the legal status of airspace. For without a precise boundary line between airspace and outer space, the status of the upper sphere of the airspace is not legally definable. This again is bound to cast a shadow on the "complete and exclusive" character of airspace. A point is likely to be reached in the future, more or less distant, where sovereignty in airspace could be safely defined as sovereignty pure and simple instead of "complete and exclusive" as it is in Article 1 of the ICAO Convention. If this stage is reached, the legal regime of airspace need no longer be an obstruction to progress from bilateralism to multilateral solutions. In fact this development has already started on a regional scale.[58] The Paris Agreement of 1956, relating to nonscheduled services in Europe, extends to regular flights for the transport of freight and for the transport of passengers between regions which have no reasonably direct connection by scheduled services. These could be classified as *residual* services, such as taxi flights with a low seating capacity.[59]

One more development in the field of international civil aviation deserves attention, namely, the impact of the International Air Transport Association (IATA) on the regime of international air services. IATA is an organization created by the leading international air lines and it is outside the domain of interstate relations. But it plays an important role through its rate-fixing machinery. IATA's unanimous decisions on fares (Traffic Conferences), backed by the governments of the countries to which the contracting airlines belong, constitute a significant contribution to uniformity of international civil aviation. Thanks to uniformity of fares combined with interline agreements and clearing arrangements, uninterrupted travel on one ticket, issued by the contracting airline, has become a workable proposition.

IATA is, in the same way as International Maritime Conferences, an instrumentality of multilateralization of services within the private (quasi-public) sector. After the failure of the Chicago Conference to organize commercial scheduled international air transport, it was IATA's mechanism that enabled, *inter alia,* the United States and the United Kingdom to work out the Bermuda Agreement and thus to establish a pattern of a bilateral transport arrangement. The bilateral model agreements usually contain a clause referring to the IATA mechanism, in the same way as they refer to the regulatory technical law laid down by the Chicago Convention. Even bilateral agreements concluded by members of ICAO with nonmembers are linked with these multilateral mechanisms.

These observations may lead to the conclusion that those responsible for defining the legal status of airspace in the Paris Convention of 1919, as well as the Chicago Convention of 1944, showed limited foresight of the developments inherent in its nature. The arguments of some of the greatest international lawyers of the period prior to World War I, such as Fauchille and Nys, were ignored while the drafters insisted on complete and exclusive sovereignty of states in airspace. It has been shown that completeness and exclusiveness are frustrated by the realities of world civil aviation. World airspace does not lend itself to a vertical division by political frontiers (in disregard of the requirements of air service control) nor can it be horizontally separated with any precision from outer space. The globality of world air transport tends to functionalize the sovereignty of states in airspace, for each member state of the family of nations acts not only as agent of its own interests but is also responsible to the community of nations for the safe and efficient functioning of the uninterrupted flow of air traffic, whether scheduled or nonscheduled (*dédoublement fonctionnel*). Premature as it may be to expect the present network of bilateral transport agreements to give way to a multilateral solution as envisaged by a number of powers at the Chicago Conference, there is nevertheless a marked tendency to an increase in uniformity of world civil aviation which in substance (though not formally) renders it cryptomultilateral. The spectacular technical developments in air navigation and the growth of world services are likely to affect, in the long run, the legal status of airspace. Its redefinition will be necessary for practical purposes of civil aviation. Perhaps the time would then be ripe for progress in the ratification of the International Air Transport Agreement of 1944.

RADIO COMMUNICATION

The discussion of the legal status of the operational area of radiocommunication presents comparatively more difficulties than the discussion of the legal status of any of the other areas of global communication. The first difficulty, one of a preliminary scientific nature, is whether we can speak at all about an operational *space* of radiocommunication. Annex 2 of the Montreux Convention of 1965 defines radiocommunication as "telecommunication by means of radio waves." Article 46 of the convention refers to the "spectrum space," but without explaining the term.[60]

If we survey the opinions of international lawyers on the legal status of the area of radiocommunication in the last fifty years, we find that they have treated problems relating to it jointly with the problems of airspace. To quote but one characteristic example: [61]

Questions relating to air navigation and to the status of aircraft are not the only ones which are connected with the employment of the airspace. Wireless telegraphy by radio waves transmitted across the atmosphere must draw the attention of lawyers. Here problems arise which relate to the rights of the States in the airspace: Is a State free to transmit from its territory radio waves which are destined to reach another State? Can a State which is between the two above States (i.e., between the State of origin of waves and the State of their destination) stop the passage of radio waves which are in transit above its territory?

If it is admitted that a State has in its airspace (atmosphere) an absolute right (be it ownership or sovereignty), it follows from this right that each State may in principle, in its discretion, send and transmit its radio waves and stop radio waves coming from neighbouring States to its territory. . . .[62]

Oppenheim, disagreeing with Fauchille, expresses the same view when he states that "the principle of exclusive sovereignty in the airspace for the subjacent State which has received general approval in connection with aerial navigation, enables that State to prohibit the disturbance of the airspace over its territory by means of Hertzian waves caused for the purpose of wireless communication and emanating from a foreign source." [63]

The logical consequences of this intermingling of the concepts of airspace and radio space are far-reaching. If it is true that frequencies (waves) travel through airspace, which therefore becomes the operational space for radiocommunication, it is also obvious that the state having sovereignty over that space has a right of extending its sovereignty to the operation of radiocommunication. Thus, in the view of authors quoted above, any state can send any frequencies from stations on its territory and any state can stop (jam) frequencies coming from abroad. If this sort of legal reasoning were brought to its ultimate conclusion, there would be no world radiocommunication and no possibility of organizing services with any measure of operational predictability.

From the legal point of view nothing would prevent sovereignty, in its application to radiocommunication, from being as complete and exclusive as it has tended to be in relation to air navigation. The only solution would be a network of bilateral arrangements and the cumbersome process of directing this network toward uniformity and potential multilateralization. While in relation to broadcasting the damage would be of limited dimensions, the deficiencies of world radiocommunication guaranteeing safety services for shipping and civil aviation, services of public correspondence, and other essential services would be disastrous.

Sir Hersch Lauterpacht suggested a remedy within the framework of international customary law when he expressed the belief that "it is possible that the growing number of treaties in this field will contribute to the more general acceptance of the principle prohibiting the abuse of rights with regard to both the emission and the passage of waves." He referred, in this respect, to the maxim *sic utere tuo ut alienum non laedas,* a general principle of the law of torts, which also became applicable in international law. Abuse of rights would occur "when a State avails itself of its right in an arbitrary manner in such a way as to inflict upon another State an injury which cannot be justified by a legitimate consideration of its own advantage." [64] Thus a state may technically act within the law but may nevertheless incur liability by abusing its rights. It would do so if it emitted waves which would unnecessarily disturb the radio space of another state or if it stopped the innocent passage of foreign radio waves.

It must again be emphasized that we are not concerned here with the contents of radio messages but only with the problem of demand and supply of frequencies which are always in short supply. ITU's concern is only with the mechanism of communication and not with what is communicated through the instrumentality of this mechanism. The violation, by injurious broadcasts originating from one state, of the public order and security of another state is a problem of general international law and not one of the law which deals with institutionalized communication within the framework of the relevant agencies (ITU).

The erroneous assimilation of the status of radio space to that of airspace by a number of international lawyers was the result, *inter alia,* of the use of certain legal terms in their colloquial sense, instead of allowing them to express scientific reality. Radio waves are electromagnetic; they spread with the speed of light and embrace the whole radio space. While airspace is filled with matter, radio space is the object of electromagnetic processes (which exist irrespective of matter) and not of mechanical ones. Radio waves travel over and below territory; they can be heard under the surface of the earth, and, what is essential, they travel to and from outer space without limitations. Thus expressions such as the disturbance of airspace over national territory by foreign radio waves give an inaccurate picture of the disturbance. For purposes of legal evaluation it would be correct to say that a radio wave sent from the territory of one state and capable of reception abroad is connected with two territorial points, namely, the point of emission and the point or points of reception. The process of transmission has nothing to do with airspace. It takes place in a similar way to light. Frequencies are not comparable to objects traveling through airspace. Aircraft can always be controlled from the ground or redirected; frequencies once emitted are beyond control.[65]

Doubt has been cast on the analogy between airspace and radio space. In the absence of such an analogy, not justified by scientific facts, there is no room for legal analogy. States have never claimed sovereignty over the radio space. In fact, it is not practically possible to divide world radio space into national sections. The frontiers of radio space are at the point of emission and at the point of reception; they cannot be compartmentalized vertically according to national frontiers. Neither can a frontier be drawn horizontally between radio space surrounding the earth and outer space. It is true that claims were made to legal title to frequencies, or at least claims to priority of use of frequencies. The relative legal controversy will be discussed below. But these claims belong to the past; ultimately they did not receive general approval.

In practical terms, insistence on sovereignty in radio space would have seriously delayed the development of radiocommunication. If states emitted radio waves from their own stations and jammed foreign waves at their discretion, utter chaos would ensue. Jamming waves travel abroad as any other wave and frustrate radiocommunication not only in the receiving country but also in other countries, including the emitting country. As mentioned above, quite apart from controversies over broadcasting which ITU was not able to solve, machinery had to be established to coordinate world radiocommunication on a reliable legal basis which, it is suggested, is the concept of *res communis* or quasi-*res communis*.

This concept was not expressly adopted in the ITU Conventions. None of them since the institutionalization of radiocommunication in 1906 (Berlin Convention) contains any provision which would define the legal status of radio space or even of radio waves. But conclusions can be drawn from certain provisions in the above conventions, particularly from those dealing with "harmful interference" and frequency registration.

Article 48 of the Montreux Convention imposes upon member states of ITU the duty to establish and operate radio stations "in such a manner as not to cause harmful interference to the radio services or communications of other Members. . . ." The text of this article indicates that *harmless* interference would not be a violation of the provisions of the convention. Annex 2 of the convention defines harmful interference as "any emission, radiation or induction which endangers the functioning of a radionavigation service or of other safety services or seriously degrades, obstructs or repeatedly interrupts a radiocommunication service operating in accordance with the radio regulations." In other words, when there is no danger to certain essential services or if the obstruction is not serious or if there is no repeated interruption, the interference is not harmful.

Thus the convention permits, under certain circumstances, the free passage of radio waves from one country to another without offense to the sovereignty of the foreign country. Moreover, Article 13 of the convention (184) refers to the members of the International Frequency Registration Board (IFRB) as to "custodians of an international public trust," which indicates the existence of a global and indivisible area of an interest-sharing nature, of common concern to all nations. The concept of *res communis,* though not expressly adopted by the convention, receives indirect support from these provisions.

The problem of the legal status of radio space is not quite comparable to that of the legal status of operational space in other branches of communication. For while in the latter international services actually operate in a physical area, the expression "radio space" cannot be interpreted in the sense of such an area but, as stated above, indicates the existence of electromagnetic processes which are instrumental in conveying messages from country to country. The medium (vehicle) of communication is the radio wave (frequency), and thus discussion of the legal status of radio space would be incomplete without a brief examination of the legal position of frequencies.

Frequencies may be claimed or used by more than one state, leading to international conflicts which disturb the smooth operation of radiocommunication. Is it possible for states to assert any legal title in relation to a particular frequency? If two or more states claim the same frequency, which of them has the better title to its use? Prima facie the principle *prior tempore potior jure* seems to offer the answer. A cursory survey of ITU practice in the past may throw some light on the problem.

ITU had introduced, in the Washington Radio Regulations of 1927, a provision to the effect that member administrations should notify the Bureau of ITU of the establishment and operation of any radio station. Member administrations also undertook to assign frequencies to radio stations in such a way as not to interfere with frequencies which had been previously notified to the Bureau. It is in this procedure that the origin of a possible principle *prior tempore potior jure* could be conceived. A number of countries advocated the conversion of the principle into a mandatory provision imposing rights and duties on member countries, but this was opposed by the United States, which objected to it on the ground that no state, administration, or station should have absolute control over the use of any particular frequency.[66] Nevertheless, after the Washington conference the ITU Bureau started publishing a list of all frequencies which had been notified by member administrations, thus bringing to the attention of the whole world the spectrum reality which no administration could ignore if it wished to enter the existing network of global radiocommunication. In order to strengthen the recording of this reality, in 1929 the Radio Consultative Committee (CCIR) called on all member administrations to notify without fail to the Bureau all frequencies in actual use. Any entry in the list comprised—apart from the details of the frequencies —the date of notification and registration.

Comparisons of dates brought the priority issue to the forefront, and a discussion on the subject followed at the 1932 Madrid Conference. The United States again objected to the formulation or recognition of any priority right connected with notification. It was generally felt that an examination of the legal aspects of frequency problems would serve little purpose. One of the committees at the conference made a statement to the effect that if two or more member administrations would submit a conflict over priority of frequencies to arbitration, the arbitral court would have to consider, *inter alia,* the following facts: the date of notification, the date of putting the frequency into operation, the power of the station, and the importance of the service carried out.[67] In 1934 the vice-director of the ITU Bureau [68] defined the possible right of priority of an administration to a frequency as a moral and not a juridical priority. In practice administrations observed the notification procedure and acted upon it, but the assignment of a frequency to actual use, in conformity with the convention and the regulations, created neither a right of ownership nor a right to priority in case other administrations claimed the frequency at a later date.

Whatever the impact of these official or semiofficial pronouncements of ITU on the law of radiocommunication, an acute controversy over the legal status of frequencies developed at the end of World War II between the United States and the Soviet Union. Before the war the ITU had compiled a comprehensive list, called the Berne List, which contained all frequencies notified by member states to the Bureau. The legal meaning of entries on this improvised register had not been clear, but when after the war ITU proceeded to reorganize the whole system of spectrum management, the Soviet Union attached exceptional significance to the Berne List, emphasizing its legal character and defending the vested rights connected with the entries in the list. This meant that the Soviet Union was upholding the principle *prior tempore potior jure,* which constituted a legalistic approach to spectrum management.[69] The Soviet Union was asserting that the priorities acquired before the war should be respected. If the picture of the frequency spectrum had changed in the meantime, it was to be brought up to date but should still be based on the Berne List. The United States objected to legal priorities or to any title to frequencies. The American argument was that the spectrum reality had changed to such an extent that no right could be attached to the former entries in the Berne List. A Frequency Allocation Table and a new Global Frequency List were needed and there was no room for legal priority. The new list would be "engineered" and problems of legal title and legal priority had to be bypassed.[70] Spectrum management was not a static affair relating to tangible objects to which legal rights and obligations could be attached. It was dynamic by nature and rather called for flexible administrative measures to achieve coordination and to avoid harmful interference.[71]

The majority of ITU members shared the American point of view, and a return to the Berne List as the exclusive basis for future frequency planning was therefore ruled out. In this connection it should be noted that the Soviet Union's legalistic approach could hardly be understood in terms of a coherent legal theory. What was really at stake was the desire to secure recognition for all the frequencies entered in the prewar Berne List and the submission of the whole new spectrum situation, as it developed during and after the war in the West, to rigid control. The Soviet Union was not yet interested in developing an international commercial radiocommunication system. Its radiocommunication was intended to be confined to its political sphere of interest, at least for the time being. Spectrum management on a static basis with undisturbed respect for the prewar distribution of frequencies was therefore suitable for this purpose. On the other hand, the unprecedented development of commercial radiocommunication in the West called for a complete reconsideration of the position, for the adoption of a new Frequency Allocation Table, a new administrative system of notification, and protection of frequencies—all based on flexible premises and not on vested rights and immutable priorities.

The difference between the two conceptions, the static and the dynamic, had important legal consequences. The adoption of the Soviet concept by ITU would have enabled states to acquire legal titles to frequencies (*jus in rem*), either by occupation or by prescription. Alternatively it would have been possible to acquire legal priority for the use of frequencies. The rejection of these concepts by the vast majority of powers made it imperative for ITU to establish an administrative system of frequency allocation and coordination. It was established by the Atlantic City Conference in 1947. We shall discuss the details of this system when examining the procedures of technical regulation.

OUTER SPACE COMMUNICATION

Reference has already been made to the legal status of outer space. It should be emphasized that outer space science and satellite communication would never have made progress without reliance on a coordinated frequency mechanism and on the use of modern radio equipment.

On the other hand, satellites offer the possibility of an unprecedented improvement of radio services, whether in the field of research for supplying meteorological information or as a relay for global communication,[72] which until now could be made only by high frequency circuits or by cable.[73] What is important for the future of commercial telecommunication on a global scale is that, thanks to satellites, point-to-point relaying of telephone and telegraph messages or direct broadcasting to the general public is possible. Press dispatches, news photos, radio bulletins, and television programs can already be relayed between continents by means of satellites. At present most of the long-distance communication channels all over the world are being used to capacity. By 1972 world communication capacity would need to increase fivefold in order to keep up with demand. Cable and conventional means of communication cannot serve the extensive number of terminals as effectively as satellites are able to do. Thus space communication is destined to supplement the conventional channels, and this seems to be possible at a lower cost than the cost of present-day services. These developments could be of particular importance to the developing areas of the world which are not linked to world centers by cable or radio. Satellite communication could provide them with links, essential for economic and social progress.[74]

While the task of defining the legal status of radio space has been fraught with considerable difficulties, which have taken much time to overcome in the teeth of protracted controversy, the definition of the legal status of outer space was consented to by the powers as soon as satellite communication became a reality. Their consent was expressed within the framework of the United Nations, in the form of the Declaration of Legal Principles (1961) and then by treaty (1966).[75]

The Declaration of Legal Principles immunizes outer space and the celestial bodies against appropriation by claim of sovereignty, by means of use or occupation, or by any other means. The declaration states that the exploration of outer space is for the benefit and in the interest of all mankind and free for exploration and use by all states on a basis of equality and in accordance with international law. In the exploration and use of outer space, states will be guided by the principle of cooperation. The treaty defines the legal status of outer space in Articles I and II and indirectly in Articles III, IV, V, and XII. The first two articles make it quite clear that national sovereignty is not extended from airspace to outer space.

It follows from the provisions of the two texts that outer space is not *res nullius* and not open to acquisition by legal title. States have not in the past made any claim to outer space; neither have they complained about violations of outer space above their territory by foreign satellites. However, semiofficial statements have been made which may cast doubt on the concept of free outer space. The vice-president of the Communications Satellite Corporation (COMSAT) spoke before the American Society of International Law about a parking space for American synchronous satellites in orbit. The concept of such a parking space is not reconcilable with the provisions of the Declaration of Legal Principles or the Outer Space Treaty, but in any case it is not likely to receive the official support of the powers.

It can be assumed that the concept of *res communis* is now a *fait accompli* in relation to outer space in the same way as it is in relation to radio space. The existence of two interest-sharing areas with similar legal status has important consequences since it makes the cooperation of two branches of communication feasible. If radio space had been legally assimilated to airspace, the coexistence of telecommunication and outer space activity would have been precarious. Legal development has made it possible to fit outer space activities into the institutionalized legal framework of the spectrum mechanism. It will be shown later to what extent the process of fitting one into the other has been successfully completed.

COMPARATIVE OBSERVATIONS

A comparison of the legal status of operational communication space in four fields of communication shows that in three of them (maritime transport, radiocommunication, outer space communication) states are faced with the problem of coordinating their services in interest-sharing areas. The position is different in the field of civil aviation in which the operational area of communication remains under the sway of national sovereignty. The legal position of the national vehicle (means) of communication entering an interest-sharing area differs from that of aircraft entering foreign airspace or territory. In the latter case the distribution of world services is at the mercy of *quid pro quo* bargaining in which each state bargains away its sovereignty in return for reciprocal concessions. This sort of bargaining across political frontiers has proved to be a stumbling block to multilateralism, which is a condition of expansion. While ICAO is called upon to deal with technical aspects of air navigation (only), the commercial organization of world air services is neither embodied in a multilateral (universal) interstate arrangement nor institutionalized, except for arrangements relating to uniform air fares which are made within the private sector (IATA).

In other fields of global communication the problems are different because national vehicles of communication travel on international routes and are outside the ambit of sovereignty. No national law holds a monopoly in interest-sharing areas of communication and the vehicles fully obey the navigational rules of international law as laid down by international agencies. This is even the case with respect to aircraft over the high seas (Article 12 of the Chicago Convention).

However, it must be admitted that while sovereignty in airspace has made world air transport bilateral, the freedom of the sea has not been able to immunize maritime transport against the threat of bilateralization, with all its restrictive consequences. IMCO has not attempted to counteract these restrictive factors, whether they be connected with the legal status of ships in foreign harbors or with government policies discriminating in favor of their own national maritime interests.

POSTAL SERVICES

The discussion of the legal status of the operational space of postal services is undertaken separately because the relevant problems are here different from those in other fields of communication. Maritime transport, civil aviation, radiocommunication, and outer space communication operate in their own specific areas. Postal services are carried out by railway, road, ship, or aircraft, and they therefore follow the principles governing inland transport, maritime transport, and civil aviation. To that extent a separate discussion of the legal status of these areas (including telecommunication by wire or cable) is superfluous. But world postal services were the first to be multilateralized and institutionalized on a global scale, through the establishment of UPU, and all UPU Conventions since the Berne Convention of 1874 contain, in Article 1, a provision to the effect that the member countries comprise under the title of UPU a single (world) "postal territory" for the reciprocal exchange of mail (letter-post items).[76]

The meaning of such a far-reaching statement, and whether it established a world territorial jurisdiction or a world postal enterprise, will be considered. Postal services have a long history. Prototypes of postal regimes were created in the great empires of the past, such as Persia, China, and particularly the Roman Empire, which had its *cursus publicus*. The Holy Roman Empire had the benefit of the Thurn Taxis organization, which started as a private enterprise but later became a quasi-public utility covering a great part of European territory. Gradually a network of bilateral postal treaties spread over the European continent and beyond, but the problems regarding postal services (and telegraphy) called for multilateral solutions. In the middle of the nineteenth century more than one hundred bilateral agreements were in force between seventeen postal administrations. In 1850 a regional Postal Union was formed in Germany, and in 1862 Montgomery Blair, postmaster-general of the United States, suggested a world conference to deal with postal services on a global scale. The conference, which met in Paris, was unable to agree on the conclusion of a treaty, but the fifteen participating states made recommendations for the adoption of certain principles by postal administrations all over the world. The Final Document of the conference contained thirty-one general principles reflecting common usage, whether usage *in esse* or *in fieri*. The ultimate conclusions reached by the conference constituted a model for the conclusion of bilateral agreements of states *inter se*. It has been shown that the situation is still the same in the field of civil aviation, where a model bilateral agreement constitutes the basis of international air transport. The general principles of the Paris Conference of 1863 found their way into the UPU Convention, which was adopted at the Berne Conference in 1874. The name of the organization at first was "General Postal Union." This Union was converted into the UPU in 1878.

The principles of the 1874 convention were formulated with such foresight that they served as the constitutional and operational basis of the organization in the next ninety years and still form the basis of the UPU Convention (Constitution) adopted at Vienna in 1964.[77] Among these principles, the establishment of a world postal territory has a dominant position.

On the issue of whether the UPU has territorial jurisdiction or whether it has created a world postal enterprise or department, the *Code Annoté* (the official commentary of the convention published by UPU) dispels any illusion. It would have been a progressive step in international law, but UPU is neither a world postal enterprise (department) nor does it have any territorial jurisdiction. Like ITU, ICAO, and IMCO, it is a regulatory agency, though its regulatory activity is not supported by sanctions which it could directly apply against recalcitrant member states. Article One of the UPU Constitution, as well as Article One of the UPU Convention, contain a guarantee of freedom of transit of mail throughout the world postal territory. Where this freedom is violated by a member state, the other member states have the right to suppress postal intercourse with such a member (Article 2 of the Convention). They have no obligation to apply sanctions, individually or collectively.[78]

The *Code Annoté* states that the expression "world postal territory" has symbolic meaning only. It emphasizes that it means the creation by UPU of uniform principles of postal services which member states are bound to include in their municipal laws (Article 22 of the Constitution). It also means the establishment of the principle of equivalence of postal charges in all member countries [79] and implies the principle of nondiscrimination, that is, nondiscriminatory (national) treatment of foreign mail by any member country.[80] A further consequence of this principle is the duty of each state to forward international mail by the most rapid route, at least the same by which it would send its own mail.

However, it would be an oversimplification to maintain that the concept of the world postal territory is exclusively symbolic. The inclusion of the principle of freedom of transit in the UPU Convention imposes a legal duty upon the territorial sovereign to concede the passage of foreign mail and other postal items through his territory. The consequences of the free transit provision deserve a more detailed examina-

tion, but in order to attempt such an examination a few preliminary ex-
planations of the UPU regime are required. One of the fundamental
principles of this regime is that of nonapportionment of postal charges
between the country of origin of mail and the country of its destination.
It constitutes one of the most significant elements in the efficient operation of world postal services.

According to this principle the postal administration of origin of
the mail keeps all the charges collected from the general public.[81] This
rule is based on the assumption that each letter sent to another country
demands a reply and that therefore the total volume of letters sent from
one country to another will be more or less the same as the volume of
letters written in reply. It is for this reason that Article 46 of the Convention of 1964, following the pattern of previous conventions, authorizes each postal administration to retain "the postal charges which it has
collected" except when otherwise provided by the convention and the
Special Agreements.[82]

It was generally estimated that elimination of all the financial difficulties of apportionment of charges between the two sets of countries
would simplify the operation of international correspondence throughout the world postal area. Proposals were made by certain countries,
particularly those which dispatch a comparatively small volume of mail
abroad and are therefore losing the expected benefits of the above
principle,[83] for the introduction of the payment of terminal charges or
costs.[84] These proposals were rejected and it was pointed out at the
London Congress in 1929 that countries which do not dispatch enough
mail and are therefore financial losers nevertheless have the advantage
of receiving a greater volume of information, whether of economic,
commercial, or cultural value. This intangible surplus is deemed to benefit its inhabitants. Thus the principle of nonapportionment included in
Article 49 is accompanied by an extratreaty principle called, in UPU
practice, the principle of balance of interest of addressor and addressee.
However, the Tokyo Convention of 1969 has modified the position by
giving deficit countries of destination a right to claim compensation
from countries of origin of the mail.[85]

As to the transit country, it is entitled to a payment from the country of origin of the mail, but the former can only require the payment of
its actual expenses connected with the carriage of mail. It cannot charge

payments of a regalian or fiscal nature (*péage*), that is, payments in consideration of allowing foreign mail into the sphere of its sovereignty. Sovereignty is not part of the bargain. Thus the right of transit which supports the concept of a world postal territory puts certain definite limitations on the territorial sovereignty of the transit country and to that extent its legal effects are certainly more than symbolic.

It may be recalled that the Vienna Congress of 1964 adopted the following resolution (C 23): "The Congress, considering liberty of transit as one of the essential and fundamental principles of UPU, appeals to the loyalty and solidarity of all member countries of the Union, to respect strictly, in all circumstances, the application of the principle. . . ." As mentioned above, the violation of the principle by a member country entitles other member countries to suppress all postal intercourse with such a member.

At the Ottawa Congress in 1957 a proposal had been made to introduce in the convention the concept of freedom of the air (for postal transport), as one corresponding to the freedom of transit in the UPU Convention.[86] Freedom of the air was meant to be the right granted to aircraft of scheduled international services to embark and disembark mail at any airport of the world where the aircraft lands in the course of its scheduled flight. This proposal aimed at a limitation of the sovereignty of member states similar to the limitations stipulated in the Five Freedom Agreement of 1944. Although the specific proposal was not found acceptable, the whole problem is now under investigation. In fact, the Vienna Congress directed the Executive Council to consider the question of the fifth freedom of the air for postal purposes and to establish contacts with other international organizations in order to carry out appropriate studies of commercial aspects of civil aviation.[87]

Another important consequence of the principle of freedom of transit, which goes beyond the limits of symbolic interpretation of the world postal territory, is the principle of secrecy and inviolability of correspondence. It may first be stated that while the UPU Constitution (Convention) expressly provides for freedom of transit and leaves the principle of secrecy and inviolability of correspondence to the area of extratreaty rules, the ITU Convention expressly provides for secrecy of telecommunication. However, it contains no express guarantee of freedom of transit, though its existence is implied in a number of articles including Articles 32 and 33. As far as transit of telecommunication by wire is concerned, the position within ITU tends to be the same as within UPU. On the other hand, secrecy of correspondence covers all branches of telecommunication including radio. Article 35 of the ITU Convention of 1965 expresses the agreement of the member states to ensure secrecy of international correspondence.

In UPU practice, an inquiry caused by a case of interception of a registered letter by a transit country in 1936 revealed the views of the majority of UPU members on the absolute respect for the principle of secrecy. The intercepting transit country pleaded that the addressee of the letter, residing in the country of destination, had been one of its nationals and had been guilty of breach of its military law and regulations. The action of this country was condemned as a violation of the principle of freedom of transit. Secrecy of correspondence seems to be a corollary of the existence of the "world postal territory." In 1939 the UPU Congress in Buenos Aires decided that "subject to exceptions provided in Article 46 no item of correspondence, open or closed, can be submitted to any control or seized." But the principle remained an extratreaty one.[88]

The effect of the outbreak of war upon the freedom of transit is dealt with in Articles 32 and 33 of the ITU Convention. The possibility of temporary suspension of services is also stipulated in Article 3 of the UPU Convention of 1964. World War I and World War II proved to be detrimental to the concept of a world postal territory, to freedom of transit, and particularly to secrecy of correspondence, which was generally suspended by the introduction of censorship in belligerent countries. But earlier there had been serious moves within UPU to oppose the imposition of restrictions on international postal services and the rights of the general public.

The records of UPU [89] show that during the Spanish-American War the United States recognized the continued validity of the freedom of transit for correspondence. The United States–Mexico treaty of 1887 contained a provision to the effect that in case of war between the contracting parties postal communication was to continue until notification to the contrary. The same type of provision had been included in the Anglo-French Convention of 1883. The opinion prevailed among writers of international law before World War I that postal and telegraph (telephone) communication would not be *ipso facto* interrupted by the outbreak of war and that such communication services persist "whenever the interests of war do not oblige the enemy to suspend them." [90] In practice the mail of neutral countries has been given protection in time of war. During the Mexican War the United States, which was occupying Vera Cruz, allowed British mail boats to pass in and out freely.[91] During the Boer War the British government did not interfere with German mail boats in South Africa. The Hague Convention of 1907 (on the Rights of Capture in Maritime War) states, in Chapter I, that mail belonging to neutrals or belligerents (official or private), found on the high seas on board neutral or enemy ships, is inviolable. If the ship is detained, the correspondence must be forwarded by the captor.[92] The inviolability of mail does not, however, exempt the neutral mail boat from search.

At the Madrid Congress of UPU (1920), twenty American states, in reaction to censorship imposed during World War I, made the following declaration, which is included in the minutes of the convention:

The respect for correspondence is a *sacred* principle, the violation of which brings *inter alia* great and unjustified harm to the whole world. We declare, in conformity with a Swiss proposal, that closed mail and open correspondence in transit are inviolable whether in territorial or maritime transit and that consequently no member country of the UPU can submit them to censorship or seize them not even in time of war.

This proposal was rejected, and secrecy of correspondence remains an extratreaty principle, with complete validity in time of peace only.

Nevertheless the view expressed in the *Code Annoté* that the world postal territory has symbolic significance only deserves some modification. It has a *sui generis* real significance which, on the one hand, gives expression to the integrational process within UPU, and, on the other, shows certain limitations imposed on member states which affect *inter alia* their exclusive territorial sovereignty. To summarize the essential components of the term, it means on the part of UPU the promotion and administration of a uniform code of postal laws and regulations of a global character.[93] Although such uniformity and the need for adjustment of municipal laws does not directly affect the territorial sovereignty of member states, the concomitant right of free transit puts definite limitations upon it. Member states are under a duty to permit the passage of mail from the country of origin to the country of destination, to respect the inviolability and secrecy of the mail even if such is in conflict with its municipal law (penal law). They are not permitted to charge the country of origin of the mail any payment of a regalian or fiscal nature but only effective expenses for transit purposes. If this is the meaning of a symbolic territorial integration on a global scale, the same term could be applied to telecommunication by wire. The position is different in the field of radiocommunication, which is governed by its own principles, as has been discussed above.

THE TECHNICAL LAW
AND THE LAWMAKING PROCESSES

《《

LEGISLATIVE AND
QUASI-LEGISLATIVE PROCEDURES

Throughout the foregoing discussion a distinction has been made between the organization of services of global communication and technical regulation. Particular attention has been drawn to the impact of the legal status of operational communication space, in each branch of communication, on the regime of services. It has been shown that postal services and telecommunication reached the level of multilateralization on a global scale and institutionalization through the creation of UPU and ITU. In most member states services in these two fields are run by governments, government enterprises, or quasi-public corporations. Uniformity of services and of technical regulation has been achieved through the integrational mechanisms of UPU and ITU.

In the field of maritime transport and civil aviation the position is different. The organization of maritime services is generally left to private initiative. IMCO has concentrated exclusively on promoting uniformity of technical regulation, mainly through initiating conventions. In the field of civil aviation the organization of services has remained on the bilateral level, and thus technical uniformity has become a problem of the highest importance. A bilateral network would be entirely unworkable without far-reaching coordination of technical standards. The ways and means of achieving such uniformity must therefore enjoy priority of discussion, particularly in view of the fact that traditional methods of treaty making have proved inadequate to meet the requirements of technical change. The pressure of progress in the field of civil aviation requires frequent modification of existing standards. Amendments must be worked out by the world civil aviation agency in order to bring about an adjustment of municipal laws and regulations in member countries without excessive delay. The traditional methods of treaty-making, which are applicable to the constituent conventions, are not sufficiently flexible to provide the necessary amendment procedure. Treaty processes require unanimous decisions. If the relevant agency is authorized to enact amendments by a majority of votes, simple or qualified, such amendments cannot escape the requirement of ratification or approval by each of the member countries. They may come into force for a majority of member states but they will not be universally binding if some member states refuse to ratify or approve them. In such a case uniformity is not achieved and the operation of international services may be complicated or in jeopardy. For this reason the first international civil aviation agency, the Commission Internationale de Navigation Aérienne (CINA), devised a new system of adjustment of technical regulation which deserves attention.

The Paris Convention of 1919 establishing CINA is composed of nine chapters which largely contain technical provisions and the details of the constitutional structure of the organization. The detailed technical rules are in Annexes to the convention. One of the most characteristic features of CINA is the conferment on the Commission of the power to amend the provisions of the technical Annexes A–G.[1] The granting of this power was tantamount to revising the technical law. The Commission was authorized to pass modifications of any of the Annexes by a qualified majority of votes.[2] The amendments became effective after notification to the contracting states.[3] The same procedure applied *mutatis mutandis* to amendments of the convention,[4] but while the latter amendments "must be formally adopted (approved) by the contracting States before they become effective," no such approval by a contracting state was required in the case of Annexes.[5] Thus a qualified majority of the contracting states [6] was able to pass amendments of technical regulations which became binding on all the contracting states without ratification or individual approval. We have here one of the rare examples of international legislation, the adoption of which has been attempted in vain by some other international organizations. It was feared that similar provisions would impede universal adherence of states to the particular international organizations.[7] The United States did not adhere to the Paris Convention of 1919 [8] since it could not delegate the power to amend technical law by extraneous legislative process, which would have compelled amendment of American law. Such delegation of legislative power to an international agency (CINA) was considered by the American government as contrary to the Constitution.[9]

An examination of the Paris Convention of 1919 shows that the first international civil aviation agency had to use a modified legal regime to keep up with the rapid technical change in the field of air navigation. It adopted a legislative pattern which replaced multilateral treaty making by a unilateral process of generating technical law. The amendments of Annexes were adopted by the governing body, the Commission, by a qualified majority of votes and became effective in relation to all member states without the need of individual approval or ratification. Since the latter was not required, it was not necessary for the governments participating in CINA to submit the amendments passed by the Commission to their legislatures. This permitted the representatives of the participating governments to debate technical problems and pass the amendments without fear of responsibility to a Parliament or other national legislature.[10] Thus it removed the whole process of the formulation of the response of the law to technical change from the orbit of politics. At least it did not allow politics to overshadow all the technical decisions which were essential for maintaining the uniformity of municipal laws in the field of civil aviation. But the price to be paid for this sort of legislative solution is universality, and CINA failed to secure global adherence. A revival of CINA or its legislative processes after World War II was, therefore, out of the question [11] since no world aviation agency could function without the participation of the leading powers, which were absent in CINA.

A modified version of the legislative process in this field has been worked out and adopted by the contracting parties to the Chicago Convention. This new process, which could be classified as quasi-legislative, also appears in a number of other agencies, particularly in WHO, WMO, and indirectly in IMCO. A discussion of the relevant comparative aspects will help to ascertain its position in the field of international law and its displacement of traditional treaty procedures. Particular emphasis will be put on the Annexes to the ICAO Convention. This discussion will also show how the regulatory legal mechanism of ICAO and other agencies responds to technical progress.

Technical law in ICAO, as well as in other organizations, takes the shape of standards or recommended practices. They are dealt with in Chapter 6 of the Chicago Convention. The ICAO Assembly has defined standards as any specification for physical characteristics, configuration, material, performance, personnel, or procedure, the uniform application of which is recognized as necessary for the safety or regularity of international air navigation and to which member states will conform in accordance with the convention. A recommended practice has the same meaning as a standard except that its uniform application is not recognized as necessary but as desirable and that member states will not necessarily conform to it but simply endeavor to do so.[12] What is meant by necessary or desirable must, for the time being, be left an open question. Special consideration will be given to it later in this chapter.

Article 37 of the Chicago Convention imposes a duty on the contracting states "to collaborate in securing the highest practicable degree of uniformity in regulation, standards, procedures and organisation in relation to aircraft, personnel, airways and auxiliary services in all matters in which such uniformity will facilitate and improve air navigation." [13] Uniformity means standardization of municipal laws and regulations in the field of civil aviation in order to make international flights feasible.

The adoption of standards and recommended practices, designated jointly as Annexes, is the task of the Council, the restricted representative (executive) organ of ICAO (Article 54,1). According to Article 90, "the adoption by the Council of Annexes described in Article 54,1 shall require the vote of two-thirds of the Council." The latter submits Annexes or their amendments (after adoption) [14] to the contracting states and they become effective within a prescribed period, unless in the meantime the majority of the contracting states register their disapproval with the Council. But even if the new Annexes or amendments become effective, a state may depart from the standards set out if it finds it impracticable (1) to comply in all respects with them, (2) to bring its own regulations into full accord with them, or (3) if the departing state deems it necessary to adopt regulations or practices differing in any specific respect from those established by one of the international standards. In such cases the departing state "shall give immediate notification to the ICAO of the differences between its own practice and that established by the international standards." Article 38 prescribes a sixty-day period for notification to the Council in case of failure to conform domestic regulations to amendments of standards.

It will be seen from the above provisions that ICAO deviates substantially from CINA procedures. While a qualified majority decision of CINA became binding on all contracting states, thus constituting an example of international legislation, Article 90 of the ICAO Convention allows a majority of states to disapprove the adoption or amendment of Annexes, and thus to render the relevant decision of the Council ineffective. Moreover, after a standard or its amendment has become effective, individual states can still depart from them.[15] However, if they do so, they must notify the council.

The council is the restricted representative body of ICAO, composed of twenty-seven members (out of more than one hundred states), and the adoption by it of Annexes or amendments, without need of ratification, is not in the nature of a treaty transaction of a multilateral character.[16] Approximately eighty states do not participate in the Council's deliberations and decision-making. Decisions are made by the Council in its role as an organ of ICAO, in other words by a unilateral act of a legislative character. But such an act is certainly less legislative than the ordinary CINA decision, for while the CINA Commission had the power to bind the minority of member states, the Council cannot do so. It is true that in both cases no individual approval or ratification by states is required for a standard or its amendments to become operative (effective). In this respect both agencies (ICAO and CINA) defy traditional treaty procedure according to which ratification is required, even if it is not expressly stipulated by the contracting states.[17] But ICAO standards or amendments may be disapproved collectively or rejected by individual states which, in such a case, have no other obligation than to notify the Council.[18] Thus the whole procedure may be styled quasi-legislative. The paradox of this pattern is the absence of "contracting in" by treaty process while allowing states to "contract out" (opt out).

Before commenting further on the above process it should be emphasized that this quasi-legislative pattern is entirely different from the legislative process by which an international organization generates its own domestic law, that is, the law governing its organs and employees. This has sometimes been called "organic law." [19] It does not directly impose duties on, or grant rights to, member states but regulates the functioning of its organs.[20] On the other hand, the quasi-legislative process relating to ICAO standards and their amendments creates rights and obligations for member states. While the latter is the outcome of delegation or transfer of regulatory power by member states to the organization, the power of the organization to pass domestic (organic) law can be conceived of as an implied power which does not require delegation or transfer of power by the member states.

As stated above, Article 38 provides for contracting out not only if a state cannot comply with a standard or adjust its law to standards but also if it deems it necessary to adopt regulations (practices) differing from standards. The latter case indicates that a member state may decide at any time to abandon compliance with an international standard.[21] This by itself would detract from the purely legislative character of standards. But it goes much further, for if a state may at any time defy a standard (original or amended), the latter's binding character would seem highly precarious. A member state cannot, of course, disregard its obligation to notify the Council if it departs from a standard. In fact, it would be possible to argue that nonnotification implies observance of a standard.[22] On the other hand, noncompliance without notification, that is, without express contracting out, constitutes a breach of the duty of notification. All member states are entitled to know about any departure from standards, since lack of knowledge may endanger the safety and regularity of air navigation. A state which suffers injury by not having received a warning about the departure of another state from a standard would be entitled to redress and to an action for breach of its obligation to notify expressly the Council of its intention to contract out. There is no room for silent contracting out in an agency which relies for the safe functioning of transport on uniformity of standards relating to the vital requirements of navigation. Standards are not only desirable, like recommended practices, but they are *necessary*.[23]

Prima facie it would seem that standards are mandatory. Such a view appears to be logical, since if notification of departure from a standard is mandatory, the very standard from which a state departs should be presumed to be of a binding nature. But it is also possible to conceive of standards as paralegal instruments which are not binding, although necessary. The observance, or rather nonobservance, of a standard by any state must be made known to all other states to enable them to register any deviation from uniformity which they might expect on the part of states, whether in relation to airworthiness, personnel, equipment, the rules of the air, or other matters regulated by ICAO standards.[24] CINA Annexes relating to these matters were mandatory, if only for the reason that they were an integral part of the Paris Convention of 1919. On the other hand, the Annexes to the ICAO Convention are not considered an integral part of the convention, although the ICAO machinery for settling disputes is available to member states in case of disagreement as to the interpretation or application of the convention and the Annexes. The ICAO Council is competent to consider these disputes (Article 84 of the ICAO Convention).

A former president of the ICAO Council has stated that the Annexes (standards) are not legally binding. In his own words: "Annexes are not to be given compulsory force. There will be no binding obligation on any nation to keep to an international standard." [25] The same view prevails generally in the literature of international air law. It should be noted that at the Chicago Conference draft Annexes were prepared to serve as models which could be acceptable to the states. Unlike CINA, where the Annexes were part of the Paris Convention and had the same force as the convention, under the ICAO regime standards are conceived as voluntary measures which may acquire mandatory force in municipal law through recognition by member states but are not binding in international law.[26]

In this connection two questions can be raised, the first concerns the usefulness of the distinction between standards and recommended practices, namely, between necessary and desirable technical regulations (considering that both are nonmandatory); the second relates to the fact that what is exhaustively regulated in the detailed Annexes is in a general way stipulated within the body of the ICAO Convention. Thus the principle of *pacta sunt servanda* would apply directly to the latter and indirectly to the former.

As to the first question, it has been tentatively argued within one or another international organization that standards, though not binding, have more weight than recommended practices. Such an argument fails to be legal since the difference between binding and not binding is qualitative and not quantitative. The legal distinction between standards and recommended practices lies with the obligation to notify departure and entails certain presumptions confined to standards. As to the second question, it must be kept in mind that, whatever may be the binding nature of general technical rules, their application in practice is determined by the details in the Annexes which are not an integral part of the convention. Moreover, the very procedure of contracting out is stipulated in the convention (while contracting in is absent), which leaves standards on the level of paralegal instruments. The validity of these conclusions can be tested by comparing ICAO standards with standards in other agencies such as WHO, WMO, and (indirectly) IMCO.

According to Article 21 of the Constitution of WHO, the World Health Assembly has the power to pass regulations relating to sanitary and quarantine requirements, nomenclatures with respect to diseases, causes of death and public health practices, and various standards and practices aiming at the achievement of the purposes of WHO. Regulations passed pursuant to Article 21 "shall come into force for all members after due notice has been given of their adoption by the Health Assembly except for such members as may notify the Director-General of rejection or reservations within the period stated in the notice" (Article 22). Moreover, the World Health Assembly has the power "to make recommendations to members with respect to any matter within the competence of the organisation" (Article 23). It follows from the above provisions that the WHO regulatory process is similar to that of the ICAO; it distinguishes between the procedure of adopting regulations (standards) and that of making recommendations, and renders the former effective (operative) for all member states without ratification or individual approval, in spite of their adoption by a majority vote.[27] It may also be noted that the above process includes the contracting out principle, and it may be recalled that the United States delegation at the constitutive meetings of WHO was largely responsible for its acceptance.[28] The delegation emphasized the need for a mechanism in the international field which would permit the rapid general application of new scientific techniques.[29]

The WHO process differs, however, from the corresponding ICAO pattern in several respects. First of all, in the case of the WHO, the Assembly (general respresentative body) is the organ which is competent to adopt standards. While all the member States participate in the WHO Assembly, in the case of ICAO the Council (restricted representative body) is the competent organ and only twenty-seven states participate in passing standards. Nevertheless, in both cases standards are adopted unilaterally and not by way of treaty procedure (that is, subject to the consent principle). They do not require approval or ratification. In the case of ICAO, however, the standards passed by the Council do not become effective if one-half of the members of the organization disapprove of them. No such restriction exists in the case of WHO.

A process different from that of the ICAO model has been incorporated in the International Sanitary Regulations adopted by WHO in 1951.[30] These Regulations enter into force for all states except for those which notify the director-general of WHO that they reject them or enter reservations. According to Article 107 of the Regulations such reservation shall not be valid unless it is accepted by the World Health Assembly. Moreover, the Regulations do not enter into force with respect to the reserving state until the reservation has been accepted by the Assembly, or, if the Assembly objects to it on the ground that it substantially detracts from the character and purpose of these Regulations, until it has been withdrawn.[31] In practice, the World Health Assembly has rejected about half of the reservations submitted by member states, and ultimately most of them were withdrawn. The Regulations have led to uniformity in world sanitary measures, to acceleration of traffic, and reduction of formalities. They strike a balance between maximum safety, which must be exercised against the international spread of diseases and minimum interference with world traffic. From the legal point of view the role of the international organization (WHO) in the quasi-legislative process and in its realization is more significant than in the case of ICAO, for the World Health Assembly, having the power to reject reservations, may put pressure on the contracting out state whenever the reservations are, in view of the Assembly, incompatible with the objectives of the Regulations. The rejection of the reservations leaves the reserving state in an awkward position by depriving it of its share in the operation of an essential international institution of considerable importance for world communication.

These comparative considerations may now be extended to WMO, which has experienced spectacular development ever since the employment of special satellites for meteorological services. Satellites carry out observations from outside the atmosphere, and they provide information promptly and on a truly global scale.[32] They contain television cameras which note cloud formations; they make radiation measurements ascertaining temperatures, and they use sensitive photometric devices which detect cloud areas. Their observations can be received continuously in any country over which they are passing, and they effect automatic picture transmissions (APT). Many countries have already adopted APT receivers (ground stations). WMO has now initiated a World Weather Watch (WWW) which is shared by all countries of the world. But the interpretation (reading) of information received from satellites, as well as from conventional sources of information, is a complex operation which requires special personnel and equipment and a supporting body of regulations.

Plans for the World Weather Watch (WWW) may be divided into three categories: (1) the global observation system; (2) the global telecommunication system (WMO is ITU's most important customer); and (3) WWW centers.

(1) Less than one-quarter of the globe has adequate meteorological stations. There is not enough information concerning the structure of the atmosphere over most of the earth.

(2) Development of telecommunication must go hand in hand with WWW. The speed and reliability of transmissions for safety services is essential.

(3) Three world meteorological centers have been established in Melbourne, Moscow, and Washington. They are equipped with high speed electronic computers and telecommunication facilities for the reception and distribution of weather data on a global scale. The centers are clearing houses for global weather information. WWW will support the weather services of member states and provide long-range forecast-

ing. A further objective may be weather modification,[33] for example, making a cloud formation produce rain or dispersing clouds or fog.

The present phase is the first in the implementation of the WWW and it provides for cooperation with ICAO (aeronautical meteorology),[34] the Food and Agriculture Organization (FAO) (projects relating to food production), the United Nations Educational, Scientific and Cultural Organization (UNESCO) (development of water resources), ITU (telecommunication problems), and WHO (human biometeorology).[35] The Fifth Congress of WMO adopted a resolution on the WWW implementation program (17 Cg-V) according to which: (1) implementation in the territories of member states should be the responsibility of the members; (2) outside national territories, that is, in outer space, the oceans, and Antarctica, the realization of WWW "should be based on the principle of voluntary participation" of countries by providing facilities and services from their national resources; (3) when national resources are inadequate, aid should be obtained from the United Nations Development Program (UNDP), and the WMO Voluntary Assistance Programme should help if implementation through UNDP is not possible; (4) the secretary-general of WMO is to negotiate agreements between WMO and member countries receiving aid.

The legal or regulatory machinery to serve WWW should be provided within the constitutional regime of WMO. What is needed is regulation for the standardization of meteorological messages. In any period of twenty-four hours, about 100,000 or more observations of weather conditions on the surface of the earth are made and thousands of observations of the upper atmosphere or of the exoatmospheric region are recorded by conventional means or satellites. They must be standardized to produce the desired result and all member countries of WMO should therefore follow the regulations which provide for uniformity of recording, processing, and distributing information.

A reading of the relevant provisions of the WMO Constitution shows that *mutatis mutandis* the same regulatory pattern has been adopted as in the case of ICAO and WHO. Regulatory powers are exercised by the Congress, WMO's general representative body, which adopts international meteorological regulations by a qualified majority of votes.[36] The position is the same as in WHO but it differs from that of ICAO, where the restricted representative body (the Council) is the competent organ. Congress Resolution No. 17 (Cg II) [37] classified the technical regulations into "standards" and "recommended practices" and decided to give them the same meaning as that of regulations annexed to the ICAO Convention.[38] Thus it is "necessary" for members to follow or implement standards, and they are characterized by the use of the term "shall" in the English text. On the other hand, it is only "desirable" for members to follow or implement recommended practices and they are characterized by the use of the term "should" in the English text. Prima facie "shall" means a legal undertaking but the same term is used in the ICAO Convention for standards, and we have seen that no legal undertaking can be read into the convention in the light of all circumstances which surround the operation of standards.

A reading of Article 8(a) of the WMO Constitution shows that "all Members shall do their utmost to implement the decisions of the Congress." [39] The further text of Article 8 (b) states:

if . . . any Member finds it impracticable to give effect to some requirement in a technical resolution adopted by Congress, such Member shall inform the Secretary-General of the Organisation whether its inability to give effect to it is provisional or final and state its reasons therefor.

The following conclusions may be drawn from the above provisions: (1) Neither standards nor recommended practices are binding on members. It is made quite clear in Article 8(a) that members "shall do their utmost" to implement Congress decisions, which excludes their mandatory effect. (2) Article 8(b) adopts the principle of contracting out by notifying the secretary-general of WMO. The submission of the notification is only legally binding in the case of standards, not in the case of recommended practices. This has been made clear in Congress decision 18 (Cg III). (3) Contracting out is not in the absolute discretion of the departing member state. The latter must give the reason for the departure. Even if this is not a legal limitation, it is a factor which discourages deviations from standards in the same way in which the WHO Assembly may obstruct reservations made by members by declaring them incompatible with WHO objectives. Thus, while the process of adopting standards is quasi-legislative, the standards are paralegal instruments only. What then is the difference between "shall" and "should" as employed in WMO texts? What has been said in this respect in the discussion of ICAO would also apply to WMO.[40]

Finally, another example of the same regulatory pattern is provided by the Convention on Facilitation of International Maritime Traffic of 1965. This is a convention adopted by an IMCO-sponsored Conference concerned with problems of facilitation, that is, with devising a program for reducing the volume of formalities and procedures for ships entering harbors and departing from them (customs, immigration, sanitary) and liberating international maritime traffic from the burden imposed by outdated municipal laws. ICAO had earlier initiated a facilitation program, the details of which are contained in the provisions of Annex 9 to the Chicago Convention of 1944. IMCO not only sponsored the Convention of 1965 but also performs important functions in its implementation.[41]

Following the pattern of ICAO, WHO, and WMO, the 1965 Convention distinguishes between measures of standards of facilitation and recommended practices. Both groups are defined in Article VI in the same way as ICAO standards and recommended practices. They are both included in the Annex to the convention, and while the former are considered "necessary and practicable in order to facilitate international maritime traffic," the second are considered desirable for facilitation. Article VIII states that any contracting government which finds it impossible to comply with any international standard in the Annex and adjust its own municipal standards in accordance with such a standard, or which deems it necessary to adopt different standards, must notify the secretary-general of IMCO of the difference between the two. Such notification should be made as soon as possible after the entry into force of the convention for the government concerned, or after the adoption of differing municipal standards. The same procedure applies *mutatis mutandis* to amendment of standards or new standards adopted in the future.[42] On the other hand, recommended practices are not immediately operative after they have been passed but the contracting governments are urged to adjust their municipal laws to them. If they do so, they should notify the secretary-general of the adjustment.

The provisions of Article VIII show that the Convention of 1965 has followed the ICAO (WHO, WMO) procedure with respect to standards. The latter are measures which become operative after their adoption by the contracting parties.[43] If a contracting government is unable to adjust its municipal law to international standards (amendments) or adopts municipal standards which differ from international standards, it must contract out by notification to the secretary-general of IMCO. If it fails to notify him, it is presumed to comply with international standards. While this quasi-legislative pattern provides a regulatory mechanism which better responds to the challenge of developments than traditional treaty procedures, the legal character of standards of facilitation is put in question again. Standards are distinguished from recommended practices by the use of the term "shall," [44] which prima facie means a legally valid undertaking. It also seems that the Annex is an integral part of the convention and that therefore the principle *pacta sunt servanda* applies equally to both. However, a study of the records of the IMCO-sponsored Conference of 1965, as far as they can be utilized for purposes of interpretation of the convention, cast considerable doubt on the correctness of such an assumption.

A proposal was made at the conference for the adoption of a separate article in the convention to the effect that "the present Convention carries an Annex which is an integral part of the (former)." The purpose of this express proposal was to link the convention and the Annex organically and to give them equal status from the legal point of view. However, it was finally dropped. Another proposal made at the conference aimed at declaring standards mandatory, independently of the legal status of the Annex, but it also failed. The chairman of one of the conference committees expressed the view of the majority of the participating states when he stated that standards in the Annex are not mandatory although they carried more weight than recommended practices. As mentioned above, this opinion ignores the difference between quantitative measure and qualitative classification and thus defies legal definition.

The records of the conference show that the participating governments viewed the whole problem in the following way: There is undoubtedly a legal duty on the part of a contracting state to notify the secretary-general of IMCO if it finds it impossible to comply with a standard (amendment) or if it adopts differing municipal standards (Article VIII). The same applies with respect to ICAO, WHO (International Sanitary Regulations), and WMO standards. If a state does not submit such a notification, it is presumed to comply with international standards, and other governments will expect it to respect all the measures stipulated in the particular standard. However, if a contracting state neither complies nor notifies, it is guilty of breach of the duty to submit a notification, and not of noncompliance with international standards.

If all the relevant instruments originating from the various agencies (IMCO, ICAO, WHO, WMO) are put into juxtaposition and compared, the same picture tends to emerge: the use of the quasi-legislative process, that is, the unilateral generation of measures by the appropriate international organ and the paralegal validity of standards. Most states participating in these agencies consider this solution helpful as establishing flexible rules of conduct. It enables states which, for one reason or another, cannot immediately adjust their municipal standards to international regulation to gain time until they are able to change their municipal laws. Thus, in the final legal analysis standards are paralegal measures which would ultimately become incorporated in the municipal laws of all member states. In the international sphere they are not legally binding but law-promoting measures which aim at uniformity and universality of adherence. Universal uniformity is essential for a mechanism of a technical and administrative nature to make global air navigation or shipping or meteorological or sanitary measures workable. The use of quasi-legislative procedures may be pregnant with jurisprudential ambiguity [45] but it might lead to the possibly general acceptance of a flexible code of conduct in the above-mentioned fields without making its operation dependent on the mandatory force of standards, and without putting excessive pressure on the adjustment of municipal laws. Perhaps it is an intermediary stage in the evolution of that part of international law which derives its *raison d'être* not from the need for the traditional, sometimes precarious, coexistence of sovereign states, but from the need of a new type of international cooperative regulation. It has gone one step further than the law evolved by UPU and ITU by endowing international organs with the power of unilateral generation of standards in preference to multilateral, often protracted treaty processes.

MARITIME SAFETY CONVENTIONS

Procedures of technical lawmaking or amendment of technical law in the field of maritime transport, postal services, and telecommunication are fundamentally different from those in the field of civil aviation. With the exception of the Maritime Facilitation Convention of 1965, which followed the ICAO pattern, the other maritime conventions recently adopted at the initiative of IMCO do not deviate from traditional treaty patterns. Thus the contracting parties to the Safety of Life at Sea Convention of 1960 [46] declared in Article I that they undertake to give effect to the provisions of the convention and of the Regulations annexed to the convention. The regulations are deemed to constitute an integral part of the main instrument. It is further stated in the above article that every reference to the convention implies, at the same time, a reference to the Regulations. The contracting parties undertook to promulgate all laws, decrees, orders, and regulations and to take the necessary steps to give full effect to the convention, and to ensure that from the point of view of safety of life a ship is fit for the service for which it is intended.

Article IX of the convention declares that it can be amended by unanimous agreement between the contracting governments, or by a two-thirds majority of the Assembly upon the recommendation adopted by a two-thirds majority of the Maritime Safety Committee, or by a two-thirds majority of a special conference.

As the detailed technical law in the Regulations is an integral part of the main text of the convention, it consequently falls under general treaty law (which applies to the convention), and its amendments are adopted multilaterally by the process of contracting in. The state which is not able to accept an amendment passed by a majority of votes may make a declaration to that effect, but such declaration must be submitted to IMCO before the amendment comes into force. Thus, there are no provisions in the convention providing for the process of opting out unilaterally. Moreover, IMCO can apply sanctions against a state making a declaration and eliminate it from the community of the contracting states. Such a state would lose all the important advantages which states guarantee to each other in the convention.

The Load Line Convention of 1966 contains provisions similar to those in the Safety of Life at Sea Convention. Article 1 of the convention states that the Annexes containing the detailed rules are an integral part of the convention. The language of this article is more definite than that of Article I of the Safety of Life at Sea Convention, according to which the Regulations are deemed to be an integral part of the main instrument.

The amendment procedure is similar in both conventions, and although states which are not liable to accept an amendment passed by a majority of votes can make a declaration to that effect, such declaration must be submitted before the amendment comes into force (Article 29). Thus, the technical law is adopted (amended) by a contracting in process in a multilateral manner, and there is no possibility of opting out unilaterally.

UPU AND ITU (REGULATORY PROCESSES)

The situation is similar in the field of amendment of the technical law of UPU and ITU. However, before a brief discussion of the relevant amendment procedure is attempted, a few observations are offered relating to the position of the regulatory law within the general scheme of the UPU and ITU Conventions.[47] Until recently both conventions were dual-purpose instruments in the sense that both contained provisions relating to the constitutional structure of the organization, as well as provisions of technical law. However, the technical part contained general provisions only, leaving the details of technical regulation to separate regulatory texts accompanying the convention. Thus the law of UPU was included partly in the convention serving as the main instrument, and partly in the Regulations, which serve as additional texts. The convention was not permanent but was revised (amended) by the quinquennial Congresses, and no state was bound by the new text without ratification. Despite nonratification by some states, the convention came into force for the states which ratified it. The adoption of a new instrument meant the abrogation of the old convention. This left non-ratifying states beyond the UPU regime. We shall see later that the concept of implied ratification was relied on to find a solution for such states and to preserve the universality of UPU. The Regulations were to be revised by common agreement at special administrative conferences,[48] but in practice it was the UPU Congress which revised both the convention and the Regulations.[49]

One of the most striking innovations introduced in the amendment procedure of UPU was the interval procedure or procedure *inter absentes*.[50] This could be started in the interval between meetings of Congresses by any member administration. Proposals for amendment were submitted to the Bureau of UPU, which circulated them among all members. A proposal became effective when it was approved by the members unanimously, by a two-thirds majority, or by a simple absolute majority. No ratification was needed, which was a significant deviation from traditional treaty practices. In spite of the requirement of unanimity in all important matters, amendments could be adopted in a number of cases by a simple or qualified majority of votes.

The whole mechanism of amendment remained in force until the Vienna Congress of 1964 introduced significant changes in the UPU organizational structure. First, it replaced the convention, which had been a dual-purpose instrument, by two instruments, namely, the Constitution, which is no longer quinquennially renewable but is permanent and contains only constitutional provisions. The Constitution is accompanied by the General Regulations, which state the rules governing the operation of the union. The convention and its (executive) Regulations contain the rules relating to international postal services and the special provisions relating to letter mail. The Special Agreements dealing with services other than letter mail are accompanied by their own Regulations. The Regulations of the convention and the Regulations of the Special Agreements are now adopted by postal administrations. Other texts (including the Special Agreements) are dealt with by plenipotentiaries of member governments. The Constitution only requires ratification. The other acts are simply approved by member states, or by member administrations. All texts can be modified (amended) by the interval (inter-Congressional) procedure, except the Constitution and the General Regulations.

The Vienna Congress brought about a constitutional split, endowing the new Constitution with separate legal status. This is a considerable improvement if compared with the pre-Vienna position. In the past, the dual-purpose instrument was submitted to periodic revision and amendment mainly for adjustment of the technical law. This dragged the constitutional part of the instrument, often unnecessarily, into the process of renewal and revision while such revision was required only from the technical point of view. The arrangement brought about at the Vienna Congress immunizes the permanent Constitution, containing the structural part only, against the renewal process. However, ratification is still necessary for the Constitution while it is not required for the other texts. Thus, the technical law of UPU deviates from traditional treaty law by requiring the simple formality of approval rather than ratification. It may be recalled that the Ottawa Congress (1957) had recommended to the Executive and Liaison Commission (now the Council) that a study should be undertaken to find a procedure by which provisions of a technical nature could be made effective more simply and rapidly than by ratification.[51] The Vienna Conference has implemented this recommendation. Moreover, as the former interval procedure is now only applicable to the technical and administrative law and not to the Constitution and the General Regulations, it is possible to bring about an amendment of certain technical texts in a legislative or pseudo-legislative way, whenever the interval procedure does not require unanimity of approval by member governments or administrations.

The position of the ITU is similar to that of UPU but subject to certain differences.[52] The ITU Convention started as a dual-purpose instrument and still remains one. A former secretary-general of ITU, G. C. Gross, stated in a paper written prior to the Montreux Convention of 1965, and containing a plan for reorganization ("The New ITU"), that most of the special provisions for radio should be transferred from the convention to the Regulations. The present Regulations could then form Annexes to the convention as do ICAO Annexes. There would be no periodical revision of the convention by the Plenipotentiary Conferences. Thus, G. C. Gross supported the idea of adopting a single-purpose convention on lines later adopted by UPU.

Although the convention still contains jointly structural and general technical provisions, the detailed technical rules have been shifted to separate regulatory texts a long time ago. These texts dealing with tariffs, codes, and other technical matters were formulated into Regulations by the 1875 St. Petersburg Conference, which annexed them to the convention.

While the convention was considered to be permanent, the Regulations were subject to periodical revision by the Administrative Conferences which, unlike the case of UPU, proved to be highly successful. In fact, they overshadowed the ITU regime and made the meetings of the plenary organ superfluous. The St. Petersburg Convention was revised in 1932 when the previous Telegraphic Union, together with the Radiotelegraphic Agency, was converted into the new International Telecommunication Union.

At present the ITU General and Administrative Regulations are divided into the Telegraph and Telephone Regulations, the Radio Regulations, and the additional (supplementary) Radio Regulations. Amendments of the convention, passed by the plenary body, must be ratified by member states, and instruments of ratification must be deposited with the secretary-general of ITU in "as short a time as possible" (Article 18 of the Montreux Convention). As to the Regulations, they were considered expressly binding according to Article 14 of the Geneva Convention of 1959. But this provision was changed at Montreux, and it is now stated in Article 15 that ratification of the convention, or accession to it, "involves acceptance of the General and Administrative Regulations in force at the time of ratification or accession." This is tantamount to upholding their binding character. Such action does not deprive any contracting state, which ratifies the convention, of the right to enter reservations at the time of signature and thus prevent ratification from extending wholly or partially to acceptance of the Technical (Administrative) Regulations. For instance, the United States delegation declared that the United States of America "does not by signature of this Convention on its behalf, accept any obligation in respect of the Telephone Regulations or the Additional Radio Regulations referred to in Article 15 of the (Montreux) Convention."

Revisions of the ITU Regulations, carried out by Administrative Conferences, require the approval of member states, which must be notified by the states to the secretary-general (Article 15,3). Thus, the

ITU regime has, on the whole, not deviated from traditional treaty procedures except for including the technical law in Annexes, separate from the convention, and not requiring special ratification of Regulations but implying their ratification from the ratification of the main instrument. While the quasi-legislative process is widely applied to the technical law in civil aviation and in one of the maritime conventions (facilitation), it does not appear within UPU and ITU. The technical law of these two agencies is adopted multilaterally by the process of contracting in, without making provision for cases of opting out, once a particular text is in force. The UPU interval procedure has certain features of the legislative process but it would be difficult to consider the adoption of amendments in the inter-Congressional period as anything else but a multilateral and contracting-in process.

The procedure of revision or amendment of the constitutional charters of the agencies of global communication does not call for separate discussion since it fits *mutatis mutandis* into the general pattern of the law of the Specialized Agencies. Modification or amendment takes place by a qualified majority of votes but the modified text must be ratified or approved. Dissenting states are not bound by the text, although this does not affect its entry into force for the states which gave their approval.[53]

ADMINISTRATIVE AND
QUASI-JUDICIAL PROCEDURES

《《○》》

THE MACHINERY OF THE IFRB

The volume of the technical law which can be found in the Conventions and in various Annexes or Regulations is so extensive that it would be difficult to attempt a discussion of the whole material. Neither would it be rewarding to do so as most of their provisions are of a highly technical nature and of special interest to technical experts rather than to international lawyers. However, some of these Annexes or Regulations contain administrative or quasi-judicial procedures which deserve the attention of the student of the law of global communication. Perhaps the most interesting and elaborate of these procedures is that of frequency registration and coordination.

The legal status of radio space has already been discussed with special reference to the controversy over legal titles in the spectrum or rights to priority of frequency use. It has been shown that ITU rejected the concept of legal title and established an administrative machinery of frequency coordination. It is within this machinery that the appropriate organ, the International Frequency Registration Board (IFRB), applies a special procedure of registration and coordination. To understand this operation the following preliminary observations are made.

World War II disrupted the activities of ITU, including its efforts to organize a system of cooperation in the field of radiocommunication.

In 1947 a conference for the revision of the Radio Regulations was held in Atlantic City. It met at the same time as the Telecommunication Conference to revise the Madrid Telecommunication Convention and the Administrative High Frequency Broadcasting Conference.[1] The first conference concerned itself with the establishment of a Frequency Allocation Table and with spectrum reorganization. It was essential to allocate frequencies to a new radionavigational service, namely, aeronautical service,[2] as well as to high frequency broadcasting. These two services called for an extensive share in the use of the spectrum. The conference drew up a new Frequency Allocation Table and reallocated the spectrum in bands to various services such as radiotelegraphy, radiotelephony, aviation, shipping, broadcasting, and defense.[3] It set up a new organ, the International Frequency Registration Board, which was to begin its normal work after reassignment of frequencies. The global allocation table also designated the great geographical regions of the world: Europe, Africa, Asia Minor, the Soviet Union, America, and Asia.[4]

To start the new Frequency Register, the Board first effected the basic registrations and the assignments resulting from the existing plans. If the Board could not obtain the necessary information, it relied on extracts from the prewar Berne List. Once this initial task was completed, the Board's next task was to keep the register up to date. The recorded frequency assignments have been published periodically in the Radio Frequency Record.[5]

The system of registration of frequencies followed by IFRB, in accordance with Article 9 of the Radio Regulations, could be summarized as follows: [6] All members of ITU who accept the Radio Regulations notify the IFRB of the assignment of any frequency to a station on their territory. The Board will examine whether the assignment is in conformity with the table and rules for allocation of frequencies, with the provisions of the ITU Convention and the Radio Regulations. It also examines whether there is a probability of harmful interference to any entry in the column of protected frequencies or to an unprotected service operating in accordance with the convention, Regulations, and table, which in fact has not caused harmful interference to protected entries. The meaning of protected and unprotected entries will be discussed later.

It has been emphasized above that the Frequency Allocation Table contains a frequency plan according to which bands of frequencies are allocated to the various services.[7] Spectrum management is carried out in two stages: (1) Collective allocation of bands to services and (2) individual assignments of frequencies by member states to their stations. It is the latter which is examined by the Board under the present procedure. Each member state has autonomy in choosing a frequency and assigning it to one of its stations, but it must act in accordance with the convention, the Regulations, and the Table of Allocations containing the frequency plan and must notify the particular frequency to the IFRB. It must do so whenever the frequency can cause harmful interference to the service of a foreign administration, when the frequency is to be used in international radiocommunication, or when an administration wishes to obtain international recognition of the use of the frequency.[8] In other words, the procedure is invoked when the assignment is not only of domestic but also of international concern.

The following are some of the details which a notification of frequencies to the board must contain: a reference to the frequency assignment, the date of putting it into use, the identification sign, the name of the particular station and the country where it is located, details about the transmitting site, the areas or regions to which radiocommunication is directed, the length of the circuit, the power in Kw, hours of operation, and other relevant details. The Board, unlike the Bureau of ITU, which, prior to World War II, dealt with frequency notifications, is an active agency which is called upon to examine notifications and which has certain quasi-judicial powers apart from its registration duties. In this respect the Board differs from another registering agency, namely, Lloyd's Register of Shipping in London, which is a passive verification agency concerned with the recording of tonnage.

The Board inquires into the completeness of each notification and if it considers the latter fit for further inquiry, it includes all the data of the notification in a circular and proceeds to the next stage, which is an examination as to conformity with the convention, the Regulations, the Frequency Allocation Table, and the rules for avoiding harmful interference.[9] The meaning of harmful interference, which is the principal object of the inquiry, has been explained above. Because no state has a legal title to a frequency or even a right of priority of usage, harmful interference, whenever it occurs, cannot be considered a violation of a right *in rem* but is a disturbance of the public order of the spectrum, which is the responsibility of ITU. The purpose of such responsibility is to avoid spectrum anarchy—hence the significance of the administrative procedure under which member states must comply with the rules of co-operation as embodied in ITU texts. These rules are treaty rules, as well as rules of international customary law, specifically the principle of prohibition of abuse of right. Treaty rights are rights in personam but they are not multilaterally or institutionally effective in the field of radio-communication. ITU, in the absence of rights in rem or effective rights in personam, attempts to avoid such anarchy by administrative measures which are applied by the Board. ITU introduced the concept of protected, as distinct from unprotected, frequencies and it will be interesting to consider what is the essence of such protection. The ITU texts do not specify the means of protection except for the entry of frequencies in the column of protected frequencies. But such entry protects a frequency only against the recording of future harmful frequencies in the register. It does not guarantee protection beyond the register to a frequency.

If the examination of a frequency notification by the IFRB proves favorable, in the sense that the frequency is found to be in conformity with the convention, the Regulations, and the Frequency Allocation Table, and is not capable of causing harmful interference to protected frequencies, it is registered in the so-called Registration Column, now called column 2a. This column contains the internationally protected frequencies on the highest level.[10] If the frequency fails in the examination, it is registered in the Notification Column, now called column 2b. In this case it would not enjoy full international protection. If a further frequency notification is submitted, the Board does not protect (administratively) the frequency in column 2b against the new frequency. However, if the unprotected frequency, in spite of being entered in column 2b, is in conformity with the convention, the Regulations, and the Frequency Allocation Table, and does not in fact cause any harmful interference to protected frequencies (notwithstanding the original likelihood of doing so), the Board will protect the unprotected frequency in column 2b against a new notification.[11] In this way there seems to be a perpetual purification of the spectrum record by the elimination of harmful elements, with the ultimate aim of entering all conforming frequencies in the protected column while forcing nonconforming frequencies into the unprotected or underprotected part of the register from which they can be rescued only if they conform and do not cause harmful interference to protected entries.

However, as mentioned above, these remarks would be subject to the condition that protection is fully effective. This seems a doubtful proposition. Although under Article 9 (611) of the Radio Regulations a station which received advice of harmful interference "must immediately cease operations," ITU cannot enforce, by normal legal procedure, the provisions of the constitutional and regulatory texts. It can only register or resist registration in a particular column, and it can decide upon the appropriate part of a column (particularly column 2a) in which to make an entry and assist the parties to an issue in their effort to claim rights bilaterally and to settle conflicts. But it cannot compel a party to modify or withdraw an obstructing frequency or its notification. However, radio space is a global and indivisible concept comprising the whole universe. It cannot be fragmented into separate areas of sovereignty, and it is not confined to the radio space of the earth with its conventional radio services. It extends to outer radio space in which frequencies are carried to and from extraterrestrial bodies. As will be seen later, the existing services, whether safety services for shipping or aviation, or outer space services guiding satellites and benefiting from them as sources of information, meteorological services, or services of public correspondence, are all intertwined to such an extent that the noncooperative behavior of any one member of the family of nations must result in chaos, anarchy, and disaster which may affect the whole world.

This is particularly so in view of the intimate interconnection between satellite and conventional radiocommunication. Since anarchy is the only alternative to cooperation, there must be self-enforcement within ITU in the same way in which it prevails within UPU, although the character of self-enforcement is different in both cases. In the case of UPU, the disregard by any state of the law of international postal services would result in self-elimination of the lawbreaker from the world postal regime, which would virtually eliminate a state from the family of civilized nations, as world postal intercourse is now part and parcel of our civilization. A civilized state has a duty to enable its citizens and residents to maintain postal intercourse with all parts of the world, and no government, whatever its political leanings, can afford to ignore the existence of the UPU regime. Here self-enforcement is of a functional nature dictated by civilization and by respect for a human right.[12] In the case of ITU, self-enforcement goes further. It is physically compelling since the adverse behavior of any state may disrupt world safety or other essential services. The only part of radiocommunication which is outside this compelling solidarity is high frequency broadcasting on which no conclusive agreement has been reached and which leads, together with television, a separate regulatory existence within the framework of its own frequency bands.[13]

The procedure of frequency registration has been discussed in an abbreviated form and calls for a few supplementary remarks. The registration of frequencies has, apart from protection, the important objective of evidencing the fact that the particular frequency is in use.[14] In principle, the register should be confined to frequencies which are in actual use, but the IFRB lost its power (which it possessed in the years 1947–1959) of deleting assignments which had not been in use for a specified period. Nevertheless the Board has, under Article 9 (516) of the Radio Regulations, powers of investigation, "using such means at its disposal as are appropriate in the circumstances," and it can cancel or amend entries in the register so that the latter "shall reflect the actual frequency usage." The Board needs the agreement of the administrations concerned to effect the cancellation or amendment, but on the other hand it will indicate in the appropriate column (13a) only the frequencies which are actually used in accordance with notified basic characteristics. This allows the Board to give an appropriate picture of actual frequency usage (517).[15] All the above functions of the Board, whether of a registering, administrative, or quasi-judicial character, justify the elevation of its members to the rank of "custodians of an international public trust," which is an area beyond national sovereignty and essentially of international concern.[16]

A few details should be added to complete this summary picture of the IFRB. The procedure of registration of frequencies contained in Article 9 of the Radio Regulations does not extend to high frequency broadcasting. The Administrative Conference held in Geneva in 1959 rejected a plan for frequency registration of bands reserved to high frequency broadcasting. But the conference established a plan for the coordination of high frequency broadcasting. Administrations submit timetables and ITU examines them to secure elimination of interference. It prepares short-term plans which are published four times a year, together with recommendations for their improvement. The administrations are not bound by the timetables, and thus the coordination plan is far from satisfactory.[17] In the frequency bands for which no international frequency list has been prepared (Nos. 600 and 603 of the Radio Regulations), dates or symbols are entered in column 2d, which offers no international protection.

As to outer space radiocommunication and its inclusion into the mechanism of IFRB, it may be recalled that the resolution of the General Assembly of the United Nations relating to outer space activity (Resolution 1721, XVI) recommended to ITU action in respect of coordination of frequency management and space communication. Following the success of Telstar, the Geneva Radio Conference of 1965 concerned itself with frequency band allocation to outer space communication and attempted the necessary revision of the ITU Regulations.[18] However, this attempt has not been quite successful. While under the normal procedure of Article 9 of the Radio Regulations, entries are made in column 2a or 2b in certain frequency bands [19] (including inter alia maritime and aeronautical mobile services), in other frequency bands [20] dates or symbols are entered in column 2d only. These are bands for which no frequency plan has been completed. Here fit the frequency bands allocated to the space service, as well as the frequency bands allocated to the fixed service or to the broadcasting service between 4,000 and 28,000 Kc/s, that is, high frequencies and the frequency bands above 28,000 Kc/s. For these bands the Master Register was built up on the basis of notices, without invoking the protective machinery of ITU. Space-service assignments follow the special procedure laid down by the Geneva Conference of 1963, which made it clear in Recommendation 9A that this is not the final solution. The details of this procedure are laid down in Article 9A. Its provisions relate to the requirements of notification, the coordination of space services with terrestrial services (but not coordination of space services inter se), and the examination of assignments by the IFRB and the registration in column 2d.

There are certain similarities between the procedures in Article 9A and the classic procedure in Article 9. In both cases the Board examines the consistency of notifications with the relevant ITU instruments, and the rules of probability of harmful interference, which is of overriding significance. But the provisional procedure in Article 9A leads to registration in column 2c and 2d only. The point is that the Geneva Conference of 1963 did not prepare a frequency plan relating to satellite telecommunication, a task which was left to the next radio conference dealing with outer space. The work of this conference (World Administrative Radio Conference, Space Communication, 1971) will be important because space radiocommunication has now advanced considerably, and apart from ITU's regulatory mechanism a new operational system has been brought into life.[21] By operational is meant the actual organization and running of commercial space telecommunication services, which rely on satellites already in orbit or to be put in orbit. The organization(s) in charge of this new system will be discussed in Chapter VII.

THE ICAO ANNEXES
AND THE IMCO CONVENTIONS

Procedures in the field of civil aviation can be found in the general technical provisions of the Chicago Convention and in the detailed technical Annexes of the above convention.[22] As we have seen, the convention is a dual-purpose instrument. It contains both constitutional and technical provisions. The significance of certain Annexes (11, 12, and 13) was discussed above within our examination of the legal status of the airspace. However, Annexes 12 and 13 deserve to be reconsidered briefly since they contain a detailed procedure relating to search and rescue services, and particularly to accident inquiries.

Annex 12 deals with the operation of search and rescue services in the territories of the contracting states, and it applies the principle of cooperation of all states concerned with such services. Special search and rescue areas are delineated by the contracting states,[23] and each of them has the duty to "take the steps necessary to facilitate the temporary entry into its territory of qualified personnel, properly accredited by the State of Registry of the aircraft required for search, rescue, investigation, repair or salvage in connexion with lost or damaged aircraft." Contracting states must assist each other regardless of the nationality of aircraft or survivors.[24]

Annex 13 contains the details of a new administrative procedure relating to aircraft accident inquiries, indicating the lessons which can be learned from such inquiries for the safety of aircraft flight. The general rules of coordination of measures of assistance for aircraft in distress are in Article 25 of the Chicago Convention. As already mentioned, the state in which the accident occurs, the Inquiry State, is the appropriate entity to institute the inquiry. The inquiry should be held on the basis of its municipal law but the latter should adopt the uniform procedure recommended by ICAO. The procedure applies only in the case of an accident to an aircraft of a contracting state occurring in the territory of another contracting State and involving death or serious injury, or indicating serious technical defect in the aircraft or air navigation facilities. The state in which the aircraft is registered (Registry State) "shall be given the opportunity to appoint observers to be present at the inquiry and the State holding the inquiry shall communicate the report and findings in the matter to that State." It is characteristic that Article 26 does not admit ICAO to the inquiry. Neither does it provide for communication of the final report to the organization which must be considered a serious gap in the ICAO provisions.[25]

The purpose of the inquiry is the investigation of the accident, the obtaining and analysis of evidence, determination of the cause, and the issuing of the final report with recommendations.[26] The Inquiry State will appoint an investigator-in-charge who should have unhampered access to the wreckage and unrestricted control over it.[27] The duly appointed participants in the inquiry are entitled to visit the scene of the accident, examine the wreckage, question witnesses, have access to the evidence, obtain copies of documents, and make submissions to the investigator-in-charge. The latter has the overall responsibility for the investigation.[28] He appoints working groups consisting of specialists in various fields of civil aviation who are concerned with the history of the flight, its details, and the causes of the accident.[29] The various groups submit their reports to the investigator-in-charge, who then prepares the comprehensive factual report of the investigation and the final analysis report.[30]

A reading of the provisions of Annex 13 shows that the procedure of accident investigation is in the nature of a quasi-judicial inquiry in which all states concerned cooperate irrespective of their national interests. Although the state in which the accident occurred is normally the Inquiry State, it should, according to Article 26 of the ICAO Convention, admit the State of Registry [31] to the proceedings, and while the article makes no reference to the State of Manufacture, the latter has, according to the provisions of Annex 13, a well-established position in the inquiry.[32]

Another type of procedure appears in the IMCO Conventions, particularly in the Convention on Safety of Life at Sea (1960), the Maritime Facilitation Convention (1965), and the Load Line Convention (1966).

The Convention on Safety of Life at Sea, which replaced the Convention of 1947, is composed of the main instrument and the Regulations. But the latter, unlike the Chicago Convention, constitute an integral part of the convention. It has been shown that they were adopted multilaterally by contracting in.[33]

Regulations 7 to 11 require initial and subsequent surveys of ships, lifesaving appliances, radio installations, hull, machinery, and other parts, and Regulation 12 provides for the issue of safety certificates for passengers, cargo, construction, equipment, and radio.[34] Certificates issued under the authority of a contracting government are to be accepted by other contracting governments unless there are clear grounds for believing that the condition of a ship, while in a foreign harbor, does not substantially correspond to the certified particulars relating to the ship and its equipment. There is obviously a presumption that it does so but it is not irrebuttable. If it does not correspond, the receiving state, and particularly its harbor authority, is not bound to accept the certificate as reflecting the conditions of the ship. The controlling officers of the receiving state must then take certain steps. They will ensure that the foreign ship does not sail until it can proceed to sea without danger to passengers or crew. If the harbor authorities intervene, the controlling officer "shall inform the Consul of the country in which the ship is registered." Moreover, the facts of the case and particularly the ship's detention must be reported to IMCO (Regulation 19). Presumably, IMCO machinery for settlement of disputes between contracting parties could be used, and no doubt the conflict would be the concern of the Maritime Safety Committee. The provisions of Regulation 19 reveal the existence of cooperative responsibility of all contracting states for the safety of all vessels belonging to any of them.

There is a far-reaching similarity between the provisions of the Safety of Life at Sea Convention and those of the Load Line Convention of 1966.[35] According to Article 3 of the latter convention, no ship to which its provisions apply can proceed to sea on an international voyage unless it has been surveyed, marked, and provided with a certificate. The convention established minimum freeboards for ships engaged in international voyages. Freeboard is the space between the upper deck and line of flotation.[36] The purpose of the convention is the establishment of uniform principles with respect to limits to which ships on international voyages may be loaded. The contracting parties undertake to give effect to the convention and the Annexes which are an integral part of it.

The issue of the certificates is within the jurisdiction of the flag (registry) state.[37] According to Article 20 of the convention, the certificate "shall be accepted by the other contracting governments. . . ." What has been said about the legal status of the certificates issued under the Safety Convention applies equally to certificates issued under the Load Line Convention. If a ship of one contracting state is in the port of another contracting state, the latter will carry out an inspection and control of the ship to verify "that there is on board a valid certificate" under the Load Line Convention (Article 21). The controlling officer will see whether the ship is loaded within the limits allowed in the certificate, and whether the ship has not been so materially altered as to be unfit to proceed to sea. Control is exercised to ensure that the ship will not sail until it can proceed to sea "without danger to passengers or the crew" (Article 21). In case of intervention (detention of the ship), the controlling authority must inform the consul or diplomatic representative of the flag state. Article 31 states that if a contracting government suspends the operation of the convention in case of hostilities or other extraordinary circumstances such suspension does not deprive the other contracting governments of any right of control under the convention over the ships of the suspending government.

With respect to the procedure contained in Article 21 of the Load

Line Convention, it should be noted that the provision speaks about the right of control, not the duty to control. But, it is submitted, the right implies a duty of controlling foreign ships since otherwise no progress would be made in perfecting standards. In the case of the Safety Convention, as well as the Load Line Convention, the task of enforcement of minimum standards is the concern of national authorities. They perform a double function, one in municipal law, the other in international law (*dédoublement fonctionnel*). Conflicts arising out of the detention of ships would be reported to IMCO, which will give publicity to any deficiency in safety standards in particular cases but cannot assume jurisdiction without voluntary submission of the issue by the parties.

The last instrument in this discussion of IMCO Conventions is the Convention on the Facilitation of International Maritime Traffic of 1965, which may be compared with Annex 9 of the Chicago Convention of 1944. The municipal laws of many countries still contain provisions relating to formalities and procedures for ships entering harbors and departing from them, which must be considered obstructive to maritime traffic. Crews and passengers often have to submit to inspections and clearances which cause delay in harbors and are an unnecessary drain on the resources of the shipping industry. The program of facilitation aims at the reduction of formalities and procedures in order to liberate world maritime traffic from the burden imposed by outdated municipal laws.[38] ICAO had earlier initiated an effective facilitation program, the details of which are contained in Annex 9 of the Chicago Convention.

Prior to the conclusion of the IMCO-sponsored Facilitation Convention, the Organisation of American States (OAS) had established a committee which drafted the Inter-American Convention on Facilitation of International Waterborne Transportation in the Western Hemisphere (1956). Subsequently, the Inter-American Port and Harbour Conference met in Mar del Plata and adopted the Facilitation Convention, briefly called the Convention of Mar del Plata.[39] However, the conference postponed consideration of an Annex containing the relevant technical law, namely, detailed standards and recommended practices relating to facilitation. In 1959, a shipping group issued a report on "Merchant shipping on a sea of red tape," and in a number of countries studies were initiated to inquire into possible programs of facilitation.[40] In

1962, the secretary-general of IMCO convened a group of experts who were asked to examine a draft convention prepared by the secretariat of IMCO. Three subgroups separately studied problems of facilitation with reference to customs' formalities, immigration, and health.[41] Precedents relating to technical regulation and procedures in other organizations were examined (ICAO, WHO, OAS). The most important pattern was ICAO facilitation, which had already achieved significant results.[42] In 1964 the expert group reached agreement on the text of the draft convention and the Annex to the convention. A special conference for the adoption of the convention was held in 1965 in London which approved the draft, subject to changes, and opened it for signature on April 9, 1965.[43]

In Article V of the convention the contracting parties undertake to adopt "all appropriate measures to facilitate and expedite international maritime traffic and to prevent unnecessary delays to ships and to persons and property on board." The facilitation provisions as laid down in detail in the Annex to the convention can be divided into those relating to the arrival, stay, and departure of ships (Article II).[44] Their purpose is to achieve "the highest possible degree of uniformity in formalities, documentary requirements and procedures" and to reduce to a minimum any alterations in them designed to meet requirements of a domestic nature (Article III). This calls for an adjustment of the municipal laws of the contracting parties to international standards, and thus a duty arises on their part to pass legislation which would bring about uniformity of standards of facilitation.[45] The legal nature of this duty has been discussed above.[46]

Following the ICAO pattern,[47] some of the standards and recommended practices in the Annex to the convention are in a negative form and some in a positive form. The negative ones require states not to impose on ships and persons more than certain maximum requirements in respect of documentation, restrictions, and control. The positive provisions require states to provide certain minimum facilities for traffic and for the convenience of passengers and crews. Whenever a question arises under negative provisions, it must be assumed that states will relax their requirements below the maximum stipulated in the standards and recommended practices. In case of positive provisions it must be assumed that states will, wherever possible, furnish more than a minimum stipulated in the Annex.

The above distinction is significant insofar as, while in both cases the interpretation of provisions must be extensive in favor of ships, passengers, and crews engaged in international voyages, it is only in the case of negative provisions that the jurisdiction of the state receiving ships in its harbors tends to be restricted. Positive provisions impose on that state a duty to provide facilities to ships but the formulation of these facilities is usually in general terms and not by precise definition. In practice the whole problem of facilitation is predominantly a negative one. Its most important purpose is to reduce documentation, restrictions, and control, and this can only be done by defining a maximum of requirements beyond which a contracting state should not go.[48] The same is the position in the ICAO Annexes. The state, which by reason of its sovereignty imposes restrictions on foreign aircraft, should not impose more than international standards allow it to impose.[49]

Certain general regulations have been defined in the Annex to the Facilitation Convention in the same way as in Annex 9 to the ICAO Convention (Chapter 8). This relates particularly to the various declarations required from ships (General, Cargo, Ship's Stores, Crew's Effects), to bonds or other forms of security required from shipowners to cover liabilities under the customs, immigration, public health, agricultural, quarantine, or similar laws and regulations of a state, and to penalties for errors in documentation. Both Annexes [50] also contain a recommended practice to the effect that the contracting states should comply with the provisions of the International Sanitary Regulations of WHO. The Annex to the Convention of 1965 states that if a contracting state is not a party to the above Regulations, its public authorities should endeavor to apply their relevant provisions to international shipping.[51] There seems to be an interconnection between the instruments dealing with different aspects of global communication which tends to secure an overall complementary globality whenever one or another state is not a contracting party to one or another of the instruments.

CONCLUSIONS

Each branch of communication has developed its own pattern of procedure. But generally speaking, two main types are distinguishable: In the first type the international function is centralized and carried out by an international organ running a mechanism of coordination and applying the administrative rules of such a mechanism. This is the case in the field of radiocommunication, with the International Frequency Registration Board in charge of an administrative system of processing notifications of frequency assignments, inquiry, and registration. It carries out administrative, as well as quasi-judicial, functions. Although the system does not enjoy the support of sanctions which could be imposed by the Board, it is in practice reasonably effective. With radio space being shared by states and with frequencies being beyond the reach of national sovereignty, the centrally guided administrative mechanism of allocation of bands and verification of assignments is the only alternative to anarchy. In these circumstances states are compelled to submit to the rules of this mechanism as far as essential radio services are concerned. To this category belong safety services in the field of shipping and air navigation, meteorological services, commercial services of public correspondence, and other services not open to the vagaries of power politics. High-frequency broadcasting and space services are still outside the protective recognition machinery of the IFRB, but efforts have been made to include space services within it.

A second type of procedure is characterized by a decentralization of the international function, often amounting to a *dédoublement fonctionnel* on the part of the contracting state carrying out the above function. When the relevant international organizations, in the absence of a centralized administrative machinery, aim at the promotion of uniformity of technical law and regulation in all the contracting states, as they do in the field of civil aviation, maritime transport, and postal, telegraph, and telephone services, they tend not infrequently to support the implementation of such uniformity by procedures which compel the contracting states to adjust their municipal laws and regulations to international standards. Such procedures may even be accompanied by sanctions if the purpose of uniformity is to secure safety of international services. Here belong the detention procedures in the Safety of Life at Sea Convention and in the Load Line Convention.

In the field of civil aviation the endorsement procedure of the ICAO Convention (Articles 39–40) could perform similar functions whenever the airworthiness of aircraft or the personnel licenses are not up to standard. But in practice, the procedure is not widely utilized.

Accident inquiry has produced its own pattern of procedure with the major responsibility upon the state where the accident occurred (Inquiry State) and without provision being made for participation of ICAO in the proceedings. The international function is also decentralized in the case of procedures to promote facilitation (maritime and air transport). Here it is not promotion of strictly uniform rules which tend to bring municipal laws into line but the uniform elimination of superfluous formalities, where maintained by the contracting states, through which the efficiency of world transport is to be increased.

TECHNICAL ORGANS
AND EXPERT DIPLOMACY

《《○》》》》》》》》》》》》》》》》》》》》》》》》》》》》》》》》》》》

THE PLACE OF TECHNICAL ORGANS
IN THE GENERAL STRUCTURE OF THE AGENCIES
OF GLOBAL COMMUNICATION

In discussing the structure of the agencies of global communication which have institutionalized the processes of technical lawmaking, it must be kept in mind that the four existing agencies came into being in two separate groups, that is, ITU and UPU in the early second half of the nineteenth century, and ICAO and IMCO after World War II. The role of ITU and UPU was that of pioneering organizations, not only in the field of communication but generally in the category of universal agencies. They were the first to establish a pattern of organs extending to the whole family of nations and of operations of a global character. It is therefore essential to recall some of the characteristic features of their formation and development, for while they started operating on the basis of international legal rules and procedures which they found at the time of their establishment, they deviated from them in the process of institutionalizing world postal and telegraph services.

It has already been shown that the regulatory activities of the agencies of global communication tend to deviate from existing treaty patterns. This applies to all agencies in this field, including ICAO and

IMCO. Attention may now be drawn to the process of establishment of permanent organs of coordination in the field of postal and telegraph services. This process was put into motion when the traditional *ad hoc* conference of representatives of states or postal and telegraph administrations was converted into the plenary organ of new agencies which was to supervise, at regular intervals, the rules of such coordination. ITU was formed in 1865 and UPU in 1874, and although their legal personality may still have been ambiguous, they acquired a separate existence in the international sphere. As to legal personality, it is important to distinguish between such personality in municipal law and in international law. While the first is now usually stipulated in constituent texts (but not in the case of UPU and ITU),[1] the second remains a matter of extratreaty concern.

The establishment of the plenary organ was accompanied by the creation of a second organ, namely, the Bureau, the forerunner of the present-day international secretariat whose affairs are the responsibility of the chief executive (administrative) officer of the agency.

The plenary organ was and is called the supreme organ (Article 14 of the UPU Constitution and Article 6 of the ITU Constitution) and it was and is composed of all member states equally represented.[2] The main functions of the plenary organ are constitutional amendment, the determination of the policy of the organization, budgetary and financial matters, and the election of the chief executive officer (ITU only). All residuary powers are by implication reserved to the plenary body. In course of time it has also assumed the power of election of members of the executive and expert organs, and of delegation of powers to such organs.[3]

The main function of the second organ (the Bureau) is to act as a clearinghouse of information in telecommunication and postal matters (Article 20 of the UPU Constitution and Article 10 of the ITU Convention). In this way a direct link has been formed between ITU and UPU on the one hand, and national telecommunication and postal administrations on the other. The information obtained and pooled multilaterally is much wider and the conclusions drawn from it are infinitely richer than any experience which could be gained by governments through bilateral channels. The Bureau is in possession of all the operational details in respect of national networks of telecommunication and postal services, the municipal laws and regulations in these fields, and any information which is essential for running these services. It is within the ITU and UPU bureaus that the pattern of an international civil service first established itself. During the first decades of its existence, although it was overshadowed by Swiss government control, from which it drew considerable benefits, and not yet protected by appropriate privileges and immunities, it had already started evolving an invaluable store of knowledge relating to global communication.

The Bureau became not only a center of information and study, it also started participating in the two important functions of financial clearing and judicial settlement by arbitration.[4] In both fields UPU surpassed other international agencies. Financial clearing was and is most important for the settlement of claims connected with postal transit for which the transit country receives payment from the country of origin of mail and of other postal items.[5] Article 101 of the Executive Regulations of the Vienna Convention maintains the traditional procedure of clearing, namely: (1) bilateral clearing of accounts between pairs of member administrations in gold francs; (2) multilateral liquidation of accounts by the Bureau, which shows (a) all debit and credit items of each administration vis-à-vis the other administrations, and (b) the ultimate debit and credit balances which a particular administration has to pay into the clearing pool, or which it is entitled to draw out of it.[6]

The conversion of ITU and UPU into Specialized Agencies of the United Nations constituted a turning point in their history. Executive (restricted representative) organs were added, called, respectively, the Executive Council (UPU) and Administrative Council (ITU).[7] While the members of the plenary body are responsible to their national governments and act under their instructions and while the organ as the supreme body is above responsibility, the members of the executive body have dual responsibility, individually to their own governments and collectively to the plenary organ.[8] This is an ambiguous solution which is far from satisfactory if it is kept in mind that the chief executive officer of the organization, who is internationally responsible, is controlled by the executive organ in his day to day work.[9] The function of supervising the Bureau, for which the chief executive officer is solely responsible, had previously been carried out by the Swiss government, but the latter lost control within the ITU, and as to the UPU, it now shares the supervising functions with the Executive Council.

With regard to the composition of the executive body, Article 102 of the General Regulations of UPU requires member states to send expert officials from postal administrations to the Council.[10] Similarly, a member of the ITU Council "shall, so far as possible, be an official serving on or directly responsible to or for telecommunication administration and qualified in the field of telecommunication services" (Article 9, 2).

It is quite clear from these provisions that the traditional diplomatic element is removed from the executive organs, which must be composed of experts working according to rules of cooperative processes. Member states which tried to ignore this state of affairs and appointed career diplomats to serve on the executive organ had to give way to the pressure of the Council concerned and change their representatives. Thus, when the Brazilian minister in Switzerland was designated as representative of Brazil on the ITU Administrative Council (1948), the Council decided that the minister did not qualify and he was only provisionally admitted. At the sixth session of the Council the latter took a similar decision disqualifying the Egyptian minister.[11] It is submitted that this sort of disqualification could not be applied by the executive organ of the ordinary Specialized Agency of the United Nations. The new technical diplomacy found its place, first and foremost, in the agencies dealing with global communication and as will be seen later, this applies also to ICAO and IMCO with the same degree of validity. The significance of this development will be examined below.

Apart from their principal organs, the agencies of global communication developed, within their structures, a number of special expert organs, some of which have risen to prominence. UPU established such an organ, namely, the Consultative Committee (Council) for Postal Studies (CCPS) in 1957 (Article 18).[12] The CCPS carries out studies and gives opinions on technical, operational, and economic questions concerning postal services (Article 104 of the General Regulations). These opinions suggest the adjustment of the law to technical change. The UPU Congress elects the thirty members of CCPS who must be qualified officials of postal administrations. According to a decision of the Vienna Congress (1964), the work of the Council is to be carried out in several sections (technical, economic, and so on). Within each section (Commission) there are working groups, and the CCPS concentrates in its work, to a great extent, on developing countries.[13]

The ITU had created similar Consultative Committees much earlier—in 1925, one for telegraphy, one for telephony, and one for radiocommunication (established at Washington in 1927). The first two committees were later amalgamated into the International Telegraph and Telephone Consultative Committee (CCITT). Each Consultative Committee of the Plenary Assembly, a Secretariat headed by a director, and study groups. The function of the committees is that of investigating technical change in the field of telecommunication. They submit their recommendations to the representative organs for working out the regulatory response to technical progress.

Apart from these expert organs the ITU structure also contains the International Frequency Registration Board, created after World War II. As stated earlier, the Board carries our registering and coordinating functions (including quasi-judicial functions), and it consists of five members elected at intervals of not less than five years by the world administrative radio conference. The members "shall serve not as representatives of their respective countries, or of a region, but as custodians of an international public trust."

The Consultative Committees (CCIR and CCITT) and IFRB require coordination with the General Secretariat, and for this purpose the coordination committee has been established (Article II). This Committee is presided over by the secretary-general and composed of the heads of the permanent (nonrepresentative) organs, namely, the deputy secretary-general, the directors of the Consultative Committees, and the chairman of the International Frequency Registration Board. If the secretary-general does not have the support of two or more members of the Coordination Committee, he may take his own decision. He must, however, report to the Administrative Council. According to Article 12, the secretary-general, his deputy, and the directors of the Consultative Committees are elected. Their staff is appointed. They are all international officials and they cannot seek or accept instructions from any government or from any other authority outside the Union. All members must respect their international status.

While the Assemblies of Consultative Committees carry out functions of technical diplomacy, similar to executive organs and Administrative Conferences, the IFRB as well as the secretary-general and the directors of the Consultative Committees and their staff are internationally responsible organs. Diplomacy is the characteristic feature of negotiating organs as distinct from the operational (administrative) actions of international organizations.[14]

The above observations are, however, subject to certain reservations with respect to the chief executive officer, who must be considered as an international technical diplomat.[15] He may not only prepare the ground for technical negotiations and assist the contracting states in their prelegislative or regulatory activities; he may also exercise the active and passive right of legation on behalf of the organization and provide a conciliatory forum for member states wishing to negotiate with the help of his secretarial machinery. He is, therefore, indirectly part of the system of technical diplomacy as developed by the agencies of global communication.

What has been said about UPU and ITU with respect to expert organs and new methods of diplomacy applies *mutatis mutandis* to ICAO and IMCO. A *sui generis* pattern of organs has appeared in the field of international civil aviation, for the progress of technical change in methods of air navigation and in transport systems requires an immediate regulatory response which, as we have seen, has assumèd the form of quasi-legislative processes. Consequently, organs have been needed to prepare and draft legislation and to pass it outside the channels of treaty procedures which are not suitable to it. This was the position within the organizational mechanism of CINA, but the latter ceased to exist after World War II, and ICAO, its successor, had to establish new organs and procedures. These were somewhat different from those applied by CINA. The process of adopting technical law changed from legislative to quasi-legislative, and though this may be considered a drawback, ICAO became a universal agency covering the whole world. The Soviet Union, which was earlier only indirectly linked to the network through bilateral channels, became a member of ICAO in 1970.[16]

The organ called upon to pass or to amend the civil aviation Annexes containing the technical law is the Council.[17] Consequently, the composition of the Council as a quasi-legislative body is of particular significance, and the election of its members has not been free from conflict. The contest between member states for representation on this type of organ is more pronounced than in agencies, such as WHO or WMO, in which the plenary organ (Assembly or Congress) retains the prerogative of passing the technical law. The same observations would also apply to IMCO, whose Council, composed of the principal maritime powers, tends to overshadow the position of the Assembly.

The procedure of election of the ICAO Council by the Assembly is laid down in Article 50 of the Chicago Convention. It requires the Assembly to "give adequate representation to: (1) the States of chief importance in air transport; [18] (2) the States not otherwise included which make the largest contribution to the provision of facilities for international civil air navigation; and (3) the states not otherwise included whose designation will ensure that all the major geographic areas of the world are represented on the Council. . . ."

Initial ICAO practice showed that states could compete for a seat on the Council in each of the three categories. Thus, if a state failed to be elected on the basis of major importance in air transport, it could be included in the category of candidates providing basic facilities for international air navigation. If it failed in this category, it could compete for a seat on the basis of geographical distribution. The constitutionality of this procedure, as laid down in Rule 57 of the Assembly Regulations, was questioned by Nicaragua at the tenth session of the Assembly. The Nicaraguan government was suggesting that the Assembly should define the principal geographical regions of the world and see to it that regions not represented on the basis of the first two categories should receive proper representation in the third category. This would also safeguard the interests of smaller and developing countries which have no chance of being elected in the first two categories. Nicaragua's argument was that if states which fail in the first two categories are allowed to compete in the third category, namely, on the basis of geographical distribution of seats, they thereby create conditions of unfair competition. It was argued that Rule 57 of the Assembly Regulations should be considered inconsistent with Article 50 of the ICAO Convention and the unconstitutionality should be removed by amendment.

The proposed amendment suggested that a state which failed to be elected in category 1 or 2 would be included in category 3 only under the condition that the geographical region to which it belongs is not yet represented by another state. Opponents of the amendment contended that Article 50 of the ICAO Convention does not vest any particular right in any particular region. The Legal Committee of ICAO disagreed with the objections to Rule 57. Subsequently, compromise solutions were attempted, and the Fourteenth Assembly of ICAO in Rome (1962) adopted the following procedure: The secretary-general publishes a list of candidate states in Council elections. States not elected in category 1 are automatically candidates in category 2. After elections in these two categories, elections are suspended for forty-eight hours. Then follows the submission of candidates in category 3. All states can submit their candidature, even if they had been candidates in categories 1 and 2. This procedure supposedly allows the Assembly to see which of the principal geographical regions are not yet represented in the new Council and to adjust the position.[19]

The performance by the Council of quasi-legislative functions requires the existence of additional organs charged with preparatory legislative work. It is within these organs that the concept of technical diplomacy and expert function tends to develop. A short outline of ICAO expert organs shows that some of them are constitutionally established while some are added to ICAO's structure extraconstitutionally. Standardization of technical law and the achievement of uniformity of air navigation and air transport throughout the family of nations requires a continuous comparative investigation of the various branches of law and regulations on a global scale. It is in this way that projects can be worked out by technical experts and lawyers for the enactment of new standards and the amendment of the existing ones. The ICAO Convention refers, in this respect, to two prelegislative organs, the Air Navigation Commission and the Air Transport Committee.[20] But while only reference is made to the latter, the structure of the former is set out in Chapter X (Articles 56–57).

According to Article 56 the Commission is "composed of twelve members appointed by the Council from among persons nominated by contracting States. These persons shall have suitable qualifications and experience in the science and practice of aeronautics." According to Article 57, the duties of the Commission are the preparation of Annexes or their amendments, to be recommended to the Council, and the establishment of technical subcommissions on which any contracting state may be represented if it so desires. Important consequences follow from the above provisions. It is obvious that preparatory work is to be carried out by the subcommissions which can be joined by any member of ICAO. In other words they may be global expert organs. Thus the spade work of technical legislation is the concern of all member states. When a matter is referred from a subcommission to the Commission, it is in the hands of a restricted and highly qualified body whose members are appointed by the Council.[21] The Commission cannot elect its president. It receives him from the Council. According to Article 57, the Commission prepares the legislative material and recommends it to the Council. The task of the Council is to pass Annexes (two-thirds majority) or amendments to them (simple majority).

Apart from air navigation meetings covering the whole area of ICAO membership, there are also regional meetings which are the expression of a measure of decentralization although they are also calculated to support the centralized efforts of the organization. There are eight regions: (1) North Atlantic, (2) European-Mediterranean, (3) Middle East, (4) Caribbean, (5) Southeast Asia, (6) Pacific, (7) South American (South Atlantic), (8) Africa and Indian Ocean. Moreover, there are regional ICAO offices in Paris, Cairo, Lima, Bangkok, and Montreal which report on cases of nonimplementation of the technical law (Annexes) by particular states. ICAO inquires whether nonimplementation is due to lack of administrative machinery in a state, lack of funds, or lack of personnel. ICAO may give assistance to member states and there may be resort to Article 70 (financing of air navigation facilities), Article 71 (provision and maintenance of facilities by the Council), and Article 74 (technical assistance and utilization of revenues).

IMCO counts among its main organs the Assembly, the Council, the Maritime Safety Committee, and the Secretariat. While the first is the general representative (plenary) body and the second the executive (restricted representative) body, the Maritime Safety Committee is the typical expert organ, comparable to some extent to the Air Navigation Commission. As stated above, the Council tends to overshadow the Assembly, a situation *mutatis mutandis* similar to that in ICAO. The Assembly elects the member countries to be represented on the Council, as well as on the Maritime Safety Committee, and Articles 18 and 28 lay down the qualification for such election. Thus the Council is composed of: (1) six states having the largest interest in providing international shipping services; (2) six states having the largest interest in seaborne trade; and (3) six states not elected under categories 1 or 2 which have a special interest in maritime transport and navigation and whose election to the Council will ensure the representation of all major geographic areas of the world.[22]

If compared with ICAO, the first two categories correspond to "the States of chief importance in air transport" or to the states providing "facilities for international civil air navigation." The third category ensures in both cases (ICAO and IMCO) equitable geographical distribution of the remaining seats.

The Assembly performs functions in technical and economic [23] matters (removal of discriminatory action and of government restrictions on shipping) but it must refer such matters to the Council for formulation of recommendations or instruments. If the Assembly does not accept the recommendations or instruments submitted by the Council, it refers them, together with its own observations, to the latter for further consideration (Article 16, h). Thus the Assembly has no power to alter the Council's recommendations. It can only send them back to the Council with its comments. As to maritime safety, the Assembly can recommend to members appropriate regulations of amendments for adoption, but they must be referred to the Assembly by the Maritime Safety Committee through the Council (Article 16, i).

The above provisions, as well as IMCO practice, reveal the special relationship between the plenary organ and the executive organ within the framework of the organization. The jurisdiction of the Assembly is strictly circumscribed by the provisions of Article 16, which also ensures a dominant role to the Council in technical as well as in commercial matters although the latter do not arise in IMCO practice. Moreover, Article 18, relating to the elections to the Council, is written in such a way as to secure a leading position on the Council for the major maritime powers. The distribution of jurisdiction between the Assembly and the Council and the composition of the latter reflect the inequality of *de facto* power in world maritime affairs.

A comparison of IMCO with ICAO shows certain similarities within the two organizations. Prima facie it would seem that the ICAO

Assembly is in a strong position vis-à-vis the Council, particularly in view of the express responsibility of the latter to the former (Article 50, a), the power of the Assembly to delegate authority to the Council (Article 49, h), as well as its controlling and residuary powers stipulated in Article 49, c and k. However, there are other factors which make the ICAO Council an organ of prime importance in the field of world civil aviation.

First of all, the Council is a permanent organ. Its president, unlike the heads of most executive organs of other agencies, is an office-bearer of international character and not simply one of the Council members elected to preside over its meetings. Articles 59 and 60, relating to privileges and immunities, equate the president of the Council with the secretary-general of ICAO, the chief executive officer, and head of the international personnel of the organization. It is characteristic that the ICAO Constitution contains no special chapter on the chief executive officer or the Secretariat. Chapter XI, which relates to ICAO personnel, refers in the first place to the president of the Council and then to the secretary-general who is appointed by the Council (Article 54).[24] Moreover, the Council draws considerable strength from the fact that it carries out the whole legislative or quasi-legislative work of the organization which establishes and amends the technical law of civil aviation. Finally, the Council has, according to Articles 54 and 55, its own mandatory and permissive functions, as distinct from delegated functions, and it appoints the members of the Air Navigation Commission (Article 56) and of the Air Transport Committee. It also defines the latter's duties (Article 54, d). Article 50 (b) makes it quite clear that the leading powers in world civil aviation should be elected to the Council. It has been shown above that efforts to change the procedure of elections in favor of the minor powers were not quite successful. Thus it would be fair to conclude that the position of the executive organ within IMCO and ICAO is not dissimilar in terms of power.

The history of UPU presents a different picture. UPU practice in the last ninety or more years has proved that the Congress of the organization was and is, in the words of the Constitution (Article 14), its "supreme organ." Its supremacy has revealed itself *inter alia* in that it has overshadowed the Administrative Conference, which is a meeting of postal administrations (Article 16). As a typical expert body the Administrative Conference should generate technical law, but it has not been allowed to do so.[25] The situation in ITU was exactly the opposite. The Administrative Conference of the organization proved to be so powerful that in the period between its formation and the Madrid Conference (1932) the plenary organ was never convened.[26] Administrative Conferences carried out the entire task of establishing and amending the technical law and regulations. The executive organs of UPU and ITU have only been brought into being after World War II, and they are not dominated by the major powers as in the case of the Councils of IMCO and ICAO.[27]

EXPERT DIPLOMACY AND THE NORMATIVE
APPROACH TO INTERNATIONAL COOPERATION

It is not intended to discuss the entire organizational structure of the agencies of global communication in detail since such a discussion belongs to a general examination of the law of the Specialized Agencies. What deserves particular emphasis is the creation of expert organs and the establishment of methods of technical diplomacy which have deviated in some way from the diplomatic tradition. In this connection the contribution made by UPU and ITU should first be recalled.

Both organizations have had to overcome the prejudices against the increase of their jurisdictional powers as voiced by many of the participating governments or administrations. It would be a fallacy to believe that the success of the two agencies can be attributed to some inherent immunity of postal and telecommunication matters to politics. There were, at the formative stage, as many objections to the curtailment of national sovereignty raised by governments as there are at present objections to the increase of the powers of other agencies such as ICAO or IMCO. Some governments objected to uniform and reduced postal rates, regarding these as a menace to national revenue policies. To this day other governments object with the utmost tenacity to the idea of abolishing postal transit rates—an idea which proved acceptable only in some of the regional Postal Unions. Insistence on priority for national considerations in international negotiations was and remains the strategy of traditional diplomacy. Its methods have hardly facilitated progress in establishing global regimes of communication. The earliest writers concerned with the development of ITU and UPU viewed "the diplomatic element . . . as a retarding influence." [28] On the other hand, experts in the field of telecommunication and postal services were less concerned with the "balancing of political interests." [29] Unlike diplomats and politicians, they gradually developed a *normative* approach (in distinction to the bargaining one) at international meetings. Their efforts usually aim at constructive cooperation in a particular technical field rather than at the preservation of the precarious coexistence which politicians try to maintain between conflicting sovereignties. Global mechanisms of communication cannot be operated without uniformity in the municipal laws and institutions of the participating countries, and such uniformity is less conceivable as a sacrifice of national authority than as promotion of everybody's interest irrespective of national sovereignty. A participating state may gain more by having a say in matters affecting all other states than by insisting on its domestic rights in isolation from other states. Technical progress in the field of communication has made the world shrink and calls for general acceptance of world standards.

The methods of traditional diplomacy may not always provide a forum through which a response of the law to technical progress can be secured. On the other hand, experts from national postal and telecommunication administrations have been aware of the disadvantages resulting from the differences between municipal laws and regulations and have been willing to influence their own governments to bring about the desirable adjustments. Important consequences have followed the growth of this new cooperative diplomacy. Technical ministries in member countries have extended their jurisdictional powers from domestic to international matters and have started participating in the completion of international technical arrangements. This has led to a change of balance within national governments and to the growth of technical ministries at the cost of foreign offices. The latter may well have kept an overall political control over affairs of international organizations but they have not had sole influence on the settlement of international technical matters.

The need for the coexistence of foreign offices with technical ministries in the administration of affairs of world communication created new patterns of competence sharing. The following were and are some of its characteristic features.[30] It was obvious that professional diplomats could not make decisions in technical matters of world communication. Because experts from the contracting states had to step in and fill the gap, foreign offices had to delegate some of their powers to technical departments to enable the latter to share in the running of international agencies. When departments or administrations in charge of postal or telecommunication services selected their delegates to international organs, foreign offices had to approve their appointment and raise them to the level of government representatives endowed with plenipotentiary or other negotiating powers. These technical diplomats received their instructions from foreign offices as well as from their own ministries or departments. In technical matters they were responsible to their own authority although in political matters they remained under the guidance of foreign offices. The category of political matter extended to various questions such as the election or appointment of high officers of international organs, the conduct of the proceedings, including voting powers, which reflect equality or inequality of states, admission of new members to the agency, expulsion or suspension of rights of members, territorial questions or problems affecting recognition of states and governments, and other similar matters. But while foreign offices still exercise primary control over technical diplomats, their competence was no longer exclusive. In questions of technical cooperation on the international level, technical diplomacy had evolved its principles and its own *esprit de corps*.

The liaison between a contracting state and the new technical international organization is maintained by the foreign office as well as by technical departments. With the passage of time the right of the chief executive officer of the international organization to maintain direct relations with technical authorities in contracting states has been expressly stipulated in a number of conventions. For example, Article 112 of the General Regulations to the UPU Constitution of 1964 states that the international Bureau "shall be at all times at the disposal of . . . Postal Administrations for the purpose of supplying them with any necessary information on questions relating to the service." The Bureau also receives requests for the conduct of inquiries directly from postal administrations. It also acts as a clearing house for postal administrations, whenever the latter seek such assistance.

Moreover, in all agencies of global communication the practice of exchanging technical documentation between the secretariat of the agency and the technical departments of member countries exists. Documentation of a political character circulates between foreign offices and the agency. This includes the invitation to a conference, its preparation, matters of credentials, signature of texts, ratification, and other matters of a similar nature. A more detailed analysis of the practice prevailing in this field would probably establish the existence of certain customary rules or usages. The principle that foreign offices have *primary* but not *exclusive* competence in dealing with the headquarters of a technical agency and must share their competence with technical authorities in their own countries can now be regarded a customary principle governing relations between international agencies and their member countries. It has, to a great extent, been developed by the practice of the agencies of global communication.

Technical diplomats are charged with the ever-increasing task of generating technical law and regulations. As shown above, they may also participate in the exercise of quasi-legislative functions. The formulation of standards by international technical organs has important consequences. Such standards do not need national approval or ratification,[31] and if so, technical diplomats are in a position to take decisions which are immediately effective for their governments. In this respect their powers exceed those of the professional diplomats who usually sign internationally agreed texts subject to the ratification of their governments. The responsibility of technical diplomats is frequently greater than that of the career diplomat.

Such responsibility is not necessarily proportionate to the professional quality of the technical diplomat, who is not likely to surpass the career diplomat in the procedural skills of international bargaining and negotiation. The exercise of functions in the interstate sphere is not the primary task of the technical expert who is an official predominantly concerned with domestic matters and affairs in the municipal field. His success in technical international agencies seems prima facie paradoxical although it comes as the result of a normative and transsovereign approach to world technical cooperation.

ARBITRATION PROCEDURES

《《《O》》》

The agencies of global communication have also carried out pioneering work in the field of institutionalized procedures of arbitration. UPU was the first world agency to formulate methods of compulsory arbitration. Settlement of conflicts within UPU takes place in two ways: in the first place, by the opinion (*avis*) issued at the request of the parties to a dispute by the Bureau (Article 112 of the General Regulations). Here the Bureau acts in a quasi-judicial role. Member states have resorted to this method of settlement of conflicts whenever they have wished to utilize a more informal process than the judicial process of arbitration. The provisions relating to arbitration are contained in Article 32 of the UPU Constitution, which states that the arbitration procedure shall apply in the event of a dispute between two or more postal administrations of member countries concerning the interpretation of the acts of the Union or the responsibility imposed on a postal administration by the application of those acts.[1]

The details of the arbitration procedure are to be found in Article 126 of the General Regulations. If a dispute arises, each of the postal administrations which are parties to the dispute selects a postal administration of a member country not directly involved in the dispute. If the respondent administration does not act on the proposal for arbitration within six months, the Bureau, upon request, calls on the former to appoint an arbitrator. After failing to get action, it appoints an arbitrator *ex officio*.

If there is a tie vote, the arbitrators should select a third administration not involved in the dispute. If they fail to agree on the choice, the Bureau appoints the third administration from among administrations not proposed by the arbitrators. Alternatively the parties to the dispute may agree to a single arbitrator, which may be appointed by the Bureau itself. It follows from the provisions of Article 126 that arbitration is compulsory.

The procedural rules applicable in arbitration cases are not laid down in the General Regulations—neither are the rules of execution of the award nor those relating to its possible revision or nullity. It is up to the arbitrators to decide upon their own rules of procedure, provided these conform with general principles of international law.[2]

With regard to ITU, settlement of disputes can take place, according to Article 28 of the Montreux Convention, through diplomatic channels "or according to procedures established by bilateral or multilateral treaties or by any other method mutually agreed upon." If none of these methods of settlement is adopted, arbitration can be resorted to.[3] The rules of arbitration are laid down in Annex 3 to the convention. They are *mutatis mutandis* similar to the rules in the UPU General Regulations. According to the Annex, however, arbitration is not compulsory because there are no provisions entitling the Secretariat to appoint an arbitrator for an uncooperative party to a dispute. Neither can the Secretariat appoint a third arbitrator if the two arbitrators cannot reach agreement on his appointment. If an agreement is not reached, each of the two nominates a third arbitrator, and the secretary-general "shall then draw lots in order to select the third Arbitrator" (para. 7).

However, changes were made at the 1965 Montreux Conference when the plenipotentiaries signed an optional additional protocol. Article 1 of the protocol makes ITU arbitration compulsory, for if one of the parties refuses to appoint an arbitrator, the secretary-general will, at the request of the other party, appoint him in accordance with Annex 3, paragraphs 3 and 4. If the two arbitrators cannot agree on the nomination of the third arbitrator, the secretary-general will intervene in accordance with Annex 3, paragraph 7.

The rules for the settlement of disputes within ICAO are contained in Chapter XVIII of its Constitution. Disputes between contracting states which cannot be settled by negotiation are, at the re-

quest of any state party to the dispute, decided by the Council of ICAO
(Article 84).[4] Any contracting state may, subject to Article 85, appeal
from the decision of the Council to an *ad hoc* arbitral tribunal or to the
International Court of Justice. If a contracting state, party to a dispute
in which the decision of the Council is under appeal, has not accepted
the statute of the International Court of Justice, and the contracting
states which are parties to the dispute cannot agree on the choice of the
arbitral tribunal, then the provisions of compulsory arbitration can be
resorted to (Article 85). They are similar to those in the UPU Constitution (General Regulations). The president of the Council will appoint
an arbitrator for the state which failed to act upon the request for arbitration. If the arbitrators cannot agree on the choice of an umpire, the
president of the Council will appoint him. The arbitral tribunal adopts
its own procedural rules and gives its decision by majority vote. The decision is final and binding (Article 86).

In the case of IMCO, questions or disputes concerning the interpretation or application of the convention are referred to the Assembly
or are settled "in such other manner as the parties to the dispute agree."
The Council for the Maritime Safety Committee may also settle questions or disputes arising during the exercise of their functions (Article
55). If a legal question cannot be settled in accordance with Article 55,
it is referred by IMCO to the International Court of Justice for an Advisory Opinion (Article 56). The International Court of Justice gave
such an opinion at the request of IMCO in the matter of the validity of
elections to the Maritime Safety Committee (see discussion in Chapter
VII).

MIXED PUBLIC
AND PRIVATE AGENCIES IN THE FIELD
OF GLOBAL COMMUNICATION

《《o》》》

The combined public and private (quasi-public) character of certain organs operating in the international field may take various forms. One is that of an entity established in private law and composed of nongovernmental entities from various countries but not empowered to take binding decisions without the participation of the interested governments. A notable example of this type of entity is IATA, the International Air Transport Association, which after World War II replaced an earlier agency of a similar character, the International Air Traffic Association established at the Hague in 1919.[1]

Another type of mixed entity has appeared in the field of commercial satellite telecommunication, namely, INTELSAT. This agency was established by intergovernmental agreement but it is composed of governments and various national corporations cooperating within the same structural framework. Still other entities, in the field of maritime communication, are either of an entirely private and national character, although performing international functions such as Lloyd's Register, or they are private international associations such as the International Maritime Committee and the International Shipping Conferences.

We have already mentioned the significance of IATA's role in world civil aviation. IATA, which is an association of international airlines, was established after World War II with headquarters in Montreal. It acquired legal personality in Canadian law by act of Parliament, which obtained royal sanction on December 18, 1945. The act recognizes IATA's international character [2] and allows it to operate outside Canada. In order to be members of IATA, airlines must run international scheduled services [3] and operate "under the flag of a State eligible for membership in the ICAO."

The above is the first link between IATA and the intergovernmental agency in the field of international civil aviation. As will be demonstrated below, such linking is an important consideration if the role of governments in IATA decisions is kept in mind. The objectives of IATA are "to provide safe, regular, and economic air transport for the benefit of the peoples of the world," a task of primary significance in IATA policy throughout the last twenty-six years. The director-general of IATA stated in his Annual Report for 1965 that "the systematic reduction in international airline fares and rates through IATA in the last 20 years has been achieved against a world-wide backdrop of rising prices and a steady decline in the purchasing power of money." IATA has not ceased in its endeavor of making air transport accessible to "the peoples of the world." [4]

In accordance with Articles VII and VIII of the Articles of Association, IATA's supreme organ, the General Meeting, meets annually and deals *inter alia* with the general policy of the organization and with budgetary questions, and elects the eighteen members of the Executive Committee. The Executive Committee elects the director-general, subject to the confirmation of the General Meeting. He is the chief executive and administrative officer of the organization. It follows from the above that IATA has generally adopted the structure of a Specialized Agency, namely, a general representative organ, a restricted or executive organ, and a Secretariat under a chief executive officer. Moreover, there are special technical organs such as the five Standing Committees.[5] Apart from the above organs there are the three Traffic Conferences which are in charge of the most important matter, the setting of fares and rates.[6]

The following is the distribution of geographical areas among the Traffic Conferences. Conference 1 covers the North and South American continents and the adjacent islands (Greenland, Bermuda, the West

Indies and the islands of the Caribbean Sea, and the Hawaiian Islands). Conference 2 extends to Europe, including the European part of the Soviet Union and the adjacent islands (Iceland and the Azores), Africa and the adjacent islands (Ascension Island), and the part of Asia lying west of, and including, Iran. Conference 3 covers Asia and the adjacent islands, the East Indies, Australia, New Zealand and the adjacent islands, and the islands of the Pacific Ocean, except islands included in Conference 1. Each of these three regions has its own requirements as to fares and rates, and if disputes arise as to qualification for membership in one or another conference, such disputes must be resolved by the Executive Committee of IATA.

The setting of fares and rates is a complicated process. Among the factors utilized to reach decisions are: the average number of aircraft employed on particular world-scheduled routes; the total flight hours less nonrevenue hours; net revenue flight hours; the average speed of aircraft; revenue in miles; the average salable capacity for the full period of operations and other factors. Among the basic elements of cost considered by Traffic Conferences are: the cost of flying operations such as crew salaries, expenses and insurance, fuel oil, and similar elements; aircraft maintenance; depreciation in flight equipment; station and ground operations such as landing charges, salaries, and wages; publicity and advertising; administrative and general office charges and capital charges such as interest and debt, income tax, and other charges. The task of the Traffic Conferences is to bring charges into relationship with costs. As mentioned above, IATA's ultimate aim is to make air transport more accessible to the general public all over the world. But it must also be kept in mind that rates for scheduled services are agreed upon as minimum rates.[7] In other words they constitute a limit below which the common carrier should not charge since this would mean unfair competition to other airlines. The more expensive carriers tend to protect themselves against the less expensive airlines, a weighty consideration if the sometimes critical (anticartel) attitude of the CAB vis-à-vis IATA decisions is taken into account. There is no doubt some substance in the CAB's objections to IATA policy, but on the other hand IATA is bound to promote compromise solutions and to avoid rate wars which otherwise would be widespread in conditions of a bilateral regime dominating the field of internationally scheduled air transport.

The situation is different from that in the field of shipping in which the profit-making policy of shipping enterprises dominates the rate-making machinery of Conferences of Shipping Lines (see Chapter I).

Each member of a Traffic Conference has one vote.[8] Action on any matter may be taken only upon the unanimous affirmative vote of the members represented at any meeting. Failure of a member who is present at the meeting to vote shall be deemed to be an affirmative vote. The unanimous decisions of a Traffic Conference must be ratified by the governments concerned [9] before they become effective. Thus a double unanimity is required to make rate decisions effective. Every airline can therefore, regardless of its size, exercise a veto. Moreover, no member airline is bound by a resolution of the conference if its government disapproves of it.[10] The fares, if disapproved even by one government, are ineffective and this may lead to an "open rate" situation.[11]

In the absence of closed fares, airlines would continue their cooperation in matters of rates along lines of informal agreement in order to make the open rate situation tolerable. In fact, IATA's Bulletin for 1966 complains that the Honolulu Conference in September, 1966,[12] which was a composite meeting of all individual and joint conferences on passenger matters, "was plagued by the growing attitude of indifference to creating open situations" and lack of compromise to close fares. The attitude of the governments to Conference Regulations was explained by the director-general of IATA in his Report for 1965: ". . . over the years less than 5 per cent of the Conference Regulations have ever been disapproved, even in part, by governments. . . ." Even if airlines were unable to agree or to secure the support of their governments, their relaxed attitude toward open rate situations would offer evidence of their conviction that rate wars cannot be risked and that cooperation is essential, whether formal or informal.[13]

Any alleged breach of conference action, such as violation of a resolution, may be reported to the director-general in the form of a complaint. Such a complaint may put proceedings of a quasi-judicial character into motion. Action may be taken by the director-general *ex officio*. If the complaint is made by a member of the Traffic Conference, the director-general forwards a copy of the complaint to the member against whom the complaint has been lodged (the respondent). This member must submit an answer to the director-general, who then refers the complaint with the answer to a Commission, or to the IATA Enforcement Office, or informs the complainant that, in his opinion, there has been no violation of the resolution. In the last case the complainant may either withdraw the complaint or request the director-general to refer the matter to a Commission. If the Commission dismisses the complaint, the complainant must pay all the costs of litigation. Even if no complaint is made, the director-general may, at his discretion, direct the IATA Enforcement Office (*ex officio*) to investigate traffic incidents coming to his attention.

Thus, IATA follows *mutatis mutandis* the pattern of practices in the field of shipping, where the application of sanctions in the case of breach of Conference Resolutions is an established tradition. In order to keep the rate situation under control, IATA has a staff of inspectors who collect information concerning rates charged by international airlines. The Breach Commission acts under IATA's Executive Committee and can impose penalties on noncomplying members. These penalties are prescribed by the Annual Meeting of IATA.[14] A member upon whom a penalty has been imposed may apply (appeal) to the Executive Committee for reconsideration of the decision of the Commission. Any penalty imposed on a member by the Commission (payable in money) is treated as a debt of the member.

Attention should also be drawn to the clearing mechanism developed by IATA, which is generally similar to the clearing pool of UPU. IATA was instrumental in bringing about an interline traffic agreement, first for passengers (1947) and later for luggage and cargo. It also worked out a universal travel plan and produced standard forms of travel documents, for example, passenger tickets and airway bills. All this allows the general public to obtain, from the contracting airline, a ticket valid for a combined international route in which other member airlines perform consecutive services on behalf of the contracting passenger. In order to deal with the highly complicated accounts which follow from millions of contractual relations between airlines and passengers, the IATA clearing house, first located in London and later transferred to Geneva, settles accounts in dollars and sterling by bringing bilateral transactions into a multilateral pool into which one airline pays its balance due to all other airlines while another airline would collect from the pool its credit balance due from all other airlines. The system exactly follows the UPU precedent established for the clearing of transit charges. To appreciate the extent of IATA clearing operations, it may be mentioned that according to the IATA Bulletin of 1966 the two-way turnover of the clearing house was 2,870 million dollars.

This brief survey of IATA provisions and practice leads to the conclusion that in many respects IATA has created a mechanism which is as effective as that built up by intergovernmental organizations. The process of rate setting in international air transport has proved to be too complex and technical to be conducted by governments. Technological advance, the expanding mass market, and competitive pressure are some of the factors which present a constant challenge to nations engaged in air transport.[15] But the policy of governments is dominated by notions of sovereignty in the airspace, which results in a network of bilateral solutions for air transport. Since vital matters of rates and fares could neither be settled bilaterally by governments nor multilaterally within ICAO (which is confined to technical matters), the initiative for a multilateral attempt to avoid rate wars had to come from the extragovernmental sphere, although governments always stand behind the contracting airlines in IATA. IATA's self-regulatory response to the challenge of world communication is one of the most outstanding in the nongovernmental sector.[16] The study of IATA's Articles of Association and its practice suggests that the organization has, for more than twenty years, been instrumental in evolving patterns of expert organs, cooperative procedures, and a type of private, technical diplomacy which required the skill of balancing the conflicting interests in the process of rate making. The above observations justify the conclusion that international lawyers, whose concern is global communication, are bound to take cognizance of the private element of cooperation as an essential factor in supplementing intergovernmental action.[17] The existence of public and private elements finds expression in the similar institutions and similar procedures working side by side.[18]

Another example of a mixed entity of a quasi-public character has appeared in the field of satellite telecommunication (INTELSAT). But unlike IATA and like the Bank of International Settlements, INTELSAT is established by intergovernmental agreement, although it is composed not only of member governments but also of national corporations acting for some of the member governments. The United States is represented by a nongovernmental corporation (COMSAT) which, apart from representative functions, also carries out managerial duties in the new organization.

This *sui generis* entity can be better understood by considering some of the antecedents of the formation of the relevant organs. Without going into technical details, the origin of the Communications Satellite Act of 1962 and its impact on satellite communication will be briefly discussed.[19]

The Communications Satellite Act is, in the view of some writers, one of the most controversial pieces of American legislation. What is particularly characteristic about it is the blending in its provisions of the influence of the public and private agencies which were instrumental in its formation. Among the private entities, the American Telephone and Telegraph Company (AT&T) had already played a considerable role in the development of satellite radiocommunication. AT&T had been responsible for the construction of Telstar I, a satellite which was placed in orbit in 1962. Moreover, AT&T has concluded agreements with communication agencies in nearly two hundred countries and areas, including Eastern Europe. It has at present about nine hundred overseas telephone circuits in operation, of which six hundred are provided by submarine cables.[20]

In the initial negotiations AT&T expressed the opinion that space telecommunication would simply be an extension of the existing conventional networks, which is quite understandable from the commercial point of view. As to the legal form of the proposed agency, it advocated joint ownership of the telecommunication system by the leading communication companies. However, since AT&T controls the bulk of international communication, there was opposition by other companies to its proposals.

The president of the United States had earlier (in 1961) made a statement on commercial satellite policy in which he accepted the idea of private ownership of the system but under the condition that such ownership and operation of private agencies would meet policy requirements of the United States administration. These included a number of essential points such as global coverage, foreign participation, nondiscriminatory access to the system, effective competition, and an economical management with low charges for services offered by private agencies. The system was envisaged as a commercial communication satellite system and as part of an improved global communication network. Some parties entirely opposed the private development of space activities but they remained in a minority. The outcome of the negotiations was a compromise between the demands of private and public interest.

Title I of the Communications Satellite Act (particularly Section 102) shows that the legal form chosen for the proposed agency was that of a private corporation (COMSAT). But it was provided that the system should be "responsive to public needs and national objectives," that it should serve the communication needs of the United States as well as of other countries, and should contribute to world peace and understanding. Further, there should be nondiscriminatory access of users to the system as licensed by the Federal Communications Commission (FCC). Thus it will be seen that the requirements stressed in the President's statement were accepted by the United States Congress. Although COMSAT is a private and profit-making entity, it also is a servant of public interest, a quasi-public entity.

Title II defines the role of the President, the National Aeronautics and Space Administration (NASA), and the FCC in the system. The President received powers of review of the system. As will be seen, the situation is *mutatis mutandis* similar to the role of the President vis-à-vis the CAB (civil aviation). The President is responsible for arrangements concerning foreign participation within the limits of the foreign affairs powers. It is also his task to assure a desirable use of the frequency spectrum. This means that he is responsible for pursuing the right policy within the ITU and particularly for securing the proper implementation of this policy by the Radio Conferences of ITU and the International Frequency Registration Board (IFRB).

The function of NASA in the system is that of a technical adviser. Unlike the President of the United States and the FCC, it has no direct control over the corporation. The powers of the United States Federal Communications Commission (FCC) are regulatory.[21] Section 401 in Title IV makes the (future) agency fully subject to the provisions of Titles II and III of the Communication Act of 1934. The FCC ensures effective competition,[22] it supervises the technical progress of the system and the sale and purchase of obligations by the (future) corporation. It can also authorize the construction, operation, and ownership of the ground terminal stations.

Title III contains the provisions relating to the creation, financing, and powers of the corporation. In matters not controlled by the Act the corporation is made subject to the District of Columbia Business Corporation Act.[23] The main organ of the corporation is the Board, composed of fifteen directors of whom three are appointed by the President, six are chosen by public stockholders, and six by communication carriers.[24] No noncarrier can hold more than 10 per cent of the voting stock of the corporation and not more than 20 per cent of the stock held by noncarriers may be owned by aliens or foreign governments. 50 per cent of the stock is reserved for purchase by authorized carriers.

Title IV designates the corporation a common carrier. The President, the FCC, and the corporation are required to report to Congress on their activities. The corporation may conduct negotiations with foreign entities and the Department of State is authorized to advise it on matters of foreign policy.

Since its establishment in February, 1963, the corporation has gone ahead with its plans for a commercial system of satellite communication.[25] It has taken advantage of the knowledge and experience provided by satellites launched for experimental purposes.[26] Telstar I, the first satellite used for international telephone and television transmissions, was launched on July 19, 1962. This satellite was designed and built by AT&T and launched by NASA. Earth stations on both sides of the Atlantic cooperated in the Telstar experiments: an American station at Andover, Maine, constructed by AT&T, one at Goonhilly Down, Cornwall, constructed by the British Post Office, and the third at Pleumeur Bodou, Brittany, constructed by the French Centre National des Etudes de Télécommunications. The experiments were successful and showed that satellites could contribute to a speedy development of global communication.[27]

Meanwhile, technical problems relating to types of orbit and types of system had been under study in the United Kingdom. The results of this study were submitted to a conference of representatives of Commonwealth governments, which was held in 1962. The conference pronounced itself in favor of the widest, and if possible global, cooperation of countries in the field of commercial telecommunication, and exploratory talks followed between the United States, the United Kingdom, Canada, Australia, and some European countries. The year 1962 saw further meetings between the interested powers (or telecommunication administrations) in Washington and in Cologne. In 1963 the participating European countries decided to form a common front, and the European Conference on Satellite Communication known as CETS was established. Among the non-European countries, Australia was associated with it. The purpose of the conference was to harmonize European views and to undertake discussions with the United States, counter-acting the bargaining position of the latter.

In the ensuing negotiations the United States, Canada, the Western European countries, Australia, and Japan participated. These countries represented more than 80 per cent of the long-distance international telephone traffic of the world. Their aim was to create an operational agency which would function side by side with ITU. The idea of entrusting the latter with operational telecommunication work in outer space was not contemplated since ITU was and is a "regulatory" body. By its nature it seems unfit to undertake the task of running an outer space telecommunication business. The term "regulatory," which is often ascribed to ITU, deserved to be in quotation marks because a typical regulatory body must have the capacity of enforcing its regulatory decisions which ITU does not really possess.[28] On August 20, 1964, the participating countries reached agreement and two interconnected agreements were opened for signature at the Department of State in Washington. These agreements entered into force the same day and the INTELSAT consortium was established.

The first of the two Washington instruments is an interstate agreement and is therefore within the realm of public international law. It sets out the general objectives of satellite communication and the applicable conditions and establishes interim arrangements for a global commercial satellite system. The second, the Special Agreement, is an operating instrument concluded by telecommunication entities which may or may not be governments. It contains the provisions regarding technical and financial cooperation.[29] As stated above, the two agreements are closely interrelated,[30] but they are two separate texts. Both agreements are of an interim character and they are intended to last only until 1971, when they are likely to be replaced by permanent arrangements.

It may be asked why was it necessary to resort to a twin agreement in the establishment of the global system. The answer seems to lie in the heterogeneity of municipal laws and institutions in the various participating countries relating to radiocommunication. Some countries have adopted a regime of public service or utility in this field while other countries have introduced competitive and profit-making institutions.[31] An example of the latter (though subject to reservations) is the United States, which, as we have seen, relies on private enterprise in the field of telecommunication. The Communications Satellite Act of 1962 reflects a blend of private and public elements, namely, the formation of a private agency subject to the control of public bodies. It created COMSAT, a private corporation with a board of mixed composition, which represents the United States in INTELSAT and is also the manager of the latter. The difficulties of reconciling these two functions will be discussed later. The system of nongovernmental organization of telecommunication in the national sphere has also been followed by some other countries such as Australia (represented by the Overseas Telecommunication Commission) or Canada (represented by the Overseas Telecommunication Corporation).[32] On the other hand, Austria, France, the Netherlands, Spain, and some other participating countries have a telecommunication organization on a governmental basis, and they are represented by their governments in the global system.[33] It has been emphasized that while the first and principal agreement was signed by governments only, the second agreement was signed either by governments or by corporations or purely private entities. But, according to Article IV(b) of the principal agreement, the participating countries are represented on the Interim Communications Satellite Committee (INTELSAT) by the representatives "from each of the signatories to the *special agreement*" and not by the signatories of the principal interstate agreement.[34]

There is a variety of representation reflecting the various municipal telecommunication systems, laws, and institutions. The global system has been introduced into the orbit of public international law through the intergovernmental character of its own constitution, the principal treaty, but allowance has been made for the diversity of municipal laws in the adoption of the second or Special Agreement. This concession has been extended to all the contracting countries which delegate governments or other entities to the organs of the system.[35] It appears that the twin agreement model provides the basis for a heterogeneous system conditioned by the variety of national regimes. It amounts to what in French legal literature is called *dédoublement des actes constitutifs*.[36] It could also be referred to as the constitutional split which, in other cases, has converted double-purpose charters into separate texts divorcing the technical and administrative provisions from the purely constitutional part dealing with the structure of the agency (see UPU).

The purpose of the formation of CETS (European Conference of Satellite Communication) by the negotiating European powers was to improve their bargaining position vis-à-vis the United States. In the course of narrowing down the issues, compromise solutions were achieved which are reflected in some of the provisions of the twin agreement. Thus, the term "global" appears in the preamble of the principal agreement but not in the text.[37] This solution, while adopting the idea of globality, allows the Europeans to make other technical arrangements outside the sphere of the twin agreement. Such arrangements could be for military or commercial purposes.[38]

The Europeans also insisted on the interim character of the agreements in the hope that by 1971, when their conversion into a more permanent system is contemplated, they would have to some extent caught up with the American telecommunication system. Some of them feel that at present they operate on conditions of inequality in view of their less advanced know-how. Fear of inequality also results from the structure of INTELSAT and particularly the voting powers of the contracting parties as laid down in the principal agreement. This point deserves careful attention.

In order to understand the distribution of votes, a few words should be said about the quota system, which has a decisive impact on voting powers. This is an arrangement which is similar to that adopted by the International Monetary Fund (IMF) and the World Bank (IBRD). According to Article I of the principal agreement, the contracting parties "shall cooperate to provide . . . for the design, development, construction, establishment, maintenance and operation of the space segment of the global commercial communications satellite system. . . ." Several phases are contemplated for the development of the system, first the experimental and operational phase during which the first synchronous satellites would be put into orbit, and then succeeding phases aiming at global coverage.

Article I explains the term "space segment" which "comprises the communications satellite and the tracking, control, command and related facilities and equipment required to support the operation of the communications satellites." [39] According to Article 3 of the Special Agreement "each signatory undertakes to contribute a percentage of the costs of the design, development, construction and establishment of the space segment equal to its quota." As to the meaning of "quota" Article IV of the principal agreement explains that it represents the percentage included in the Annex to the Special Agreement and set forth opposite the names of the signatories to the agreements. Thus, the United States, the leading outer space power, has a quota of 61 per cent, the United Kingdom has 8.4 per cent, France and Germany each have 6.1 per cent, Canada has 3.7 per cent, and Australia 2.75 per cent. Other countries have similar quotas, the last among the founder members being the Vatican City with 0.05 per cent.[40] As in the case of IMF and IBRD, the quotas determine the contributions of the contracting countries to the common pool of the organization, the currency pool, or the space segment, and they also determine the voting rights of the parties. The distribution of these rights is laid down in Article V of the principal agreement.

According to the above article, "Each signatory to the Special Agreement or group of signatories to the Special Agreement represented on the Committee shall have a number of votes equal to its quota, or to their combined quotas, as the case may be." The reason for combining quotas is explained in Article IV according to which the Committee is composed of "one representative from each of the signatories of the Special Agreement whose quota is not less than 1.5%, and one representative from any two or more signatories to the Special Agreement whose combined quotas total not less than 1.5%. . . ."— hence the need for the countries in the lower part of the quota list to combine for the purpose of obtaining the right to vote.

This distribution of voting rights may remind us of the situation in the IMF and IBRD, but it is different from the latter as no one country in the IMF or in the IBRD has a quota of more than 50 per cent and is able to establish an automatic *fait accompli* by a majority of votes. This, however, is possible in INTELSAT in which, as we have seen, the United States has an initial quota of 61 per cent. This quota has now been decreased because of the accession of new members,[41] but it is still more than 50 per cent and remains so constitutionally. This situation has been partially corrected in Article V of the principal agreement by the introduction of a qualified majority for some of the more important decisions, but there is still a residue of matters in which a simple majority of votes would be sufficient, and in which no voting is actually necessary since the leading power has a constitutionally guaranteed majority. As a result certain writers have classified the agreement as an unequal treaty, a term which dates back to the period of the classical law of nations.[42]

Inequality in treaty provision is, of course, the expression of *de facto* power inequality, which is the present situation in the field of satellite communication. However, the provisions of Article V advocate unanimity, a solution which, as we have seen, has been followed in the practice of UPU.[43] If unanimity is not obtainable and a decision is to be taken in a matter of importance (as laid down in point c), then a qualified majority of votes is required. A decision in this category "must have the concurrence of representatives whose total votes exceed the vote of the representative with the largest vote (the United States) by not less than 12.5 per cent." Among matters requiring such a qualified majority are the choice of type or types of space segment to be established, establishment of general standards for approval of earth stations for access to the space segment, approval of budget by major categories, approval of quotas and other matters of a financial and technical nature or relating to amendment or withdrawal.

Whenever the Committee is unable to take a decision in the matter of choice of type or types of space segment to be established (Vc) [44], a new attempt may be made to make such decisions by the concurring votes of representatives whose total votes exceed the vote of the representative with the largest vote by no less than 8.5 per cent.[45] Thus, initially the qualified majority was 61 plus 12.5, or 73.5 per cent, and if such majority could not be achieved, it was in certain cases 61 plus 8.5, or, 69.5 per cent. These percentages have now, after the accession of new members, decreased proportionately. In this connection Article XII states that the agreement is open for signature to all members of ITU, that is, practically to all members of the family of nations, except East Germany, North Vietnam, and North Korea. When additional states became parties to the agreement, quotas were assigned to them and this affected the quotas of the existing signatories. But according to Article XII(c) the combined original quotas of the new signatories, that is, states other than those listed in the Annex of the Special Agreement, must not exceed 17 per cent. More than forty new states have become parties to the two agreements, in addition to the original members.[46]

In connection with the increase of membership, the quota of the United States fell in 1965 from 61 to 58.57 per cent and in 1967 to 53.8.[47] Thus, the qualified majority provided in Article V is now 66.3 or 62.3 per cent. But whatever the number of new signatories (which is likely to increase), they can never have more than 17 per cent in the aggregate. This is a provision of doubtful usefulness if it is realized that the whole system is planned to be global and should ultimately extend to all members of ITU. It is quite obvious that when the interim arrangement is converted into a permanent system in 1971, the amendment of the quota system should be given serious consideration. The above discussion may help to throw some light on the view expressed by some writers to the effect that the two agreements can be classified as unequal treaties.[48]

The Soviet Union has heavily criticized INTELSAT at some of the meetings of the United Nations Committee on the Peaceful Use of Outer Space.[49] It expressed the view that the two agreements are not consistent with the Resolutions of the Central Assembly on Outer Space and that the private and profit-making character of COMSAT cannot be reconciled with the responsibilities of states for all activities in outer space. Moreover, the Soviet Union also pointed out that the voting procedures of INTELSAT are offensive to the principle of sovereign equality of states. While the first objection seems to have lost much validity after the adoption of the Outer Space Treaty, the second one is of more serious nature, at least in view of the fact that INTELSAT was planned to be a global entity with the participation of all members of ITU. As time goes on, it may be increasingly difficult to differentiate between membership in the regulatory and in the operational field of global radiocommunication. As to objections relating to voting power, adjustment in the provisions regulating the distribution of votes seem advisable. Setting 17 per cent of additional quotas for all new members is obviously not sufficient to accommodate the remainder of the family of nations in INTELSAT.[50] Nevertheless, Soviet criticism aimed at the principle of weighted voting is not justified since many agencies have adopted this kind of voting to give proper expression to differences in economic and technical power. This would not only apply to IMF and IBRD but also to most of the International Commodity Councils.

Criticism has also been directed against INTELSAT on account of the fact that the contracting countries with quotas smaller than 1.5 per cent are unable to vote unless they combine and establish voting groups representing more than 1.5 per cent. In fact, it is pointed out that at various periods a certain percentage of countries who were unable to form combined voting groups were entirely deprived of their right to vote.[51] Deplorable as this may be, it is not attributable to any defect in the constitutional provisions of INTELSAT, but it seems rather to be the consequence of the inability or unwillingness of some of the smaller countries to form suitable voting groups.

More serious is the objection that COMSAT both represents the United States and is one of the organs of the system. While the Committee is the governing body of INTELSAT and has, according to Article IV of the principal agreement, "responsibility for the design, development, construction, establishment, maintenance and operation of the space segment of the system" and exercises "the function and . . . the powers set forth in (the) agreement and in the special agreement," COMSAT acts according to Article VIII as the manager of the system. The roles of the two organs are thus divided in such a way that, while COMSAT is the managerial organ for the performance of the functions enumerated in Articles IV and VIII, the Committee of INTELSAT has the ultimate responsibility for carrying out these functions. But COMSAT figures in the list annexed to the Special Agreement as the signatory for the United States and is the representative of the latter in the system. Thus, COMSAT is at the same time in the role of a controlling and of a controlled agency and the question arises whether COMSAT's two functions are reconcilable.

In the foregoing discussion of the American Communications Satellite Act of 1962, the role of COMSAT, the President, Congress,

NASA, FCC, and the corporation in the implementation of the act have been examined. The corporation is subject to the District of Columbia Business Act and the composition of its board shows the joint influence of the President, the participating common carriers (particularly AT&T), and the stockholders. The FCC has control over the decisions of the corporation but the latter, as manager of the international system, must look to the INTELSAT Committee for approval of certain important decisions, to mention only those taken under Article 10 of the Special Agreement, namely, the placing of contracts for design, development and procurement of equipment for the space segment.[52] The reconciling of instructions received by COMSAT from its home authorities with those received from the International Committee may not always be a simple matter. COMSAT's shareholders are interested in profit making while INTELSAT's objective is to provide global and nondiscriminatory services to the general public at low rates. In this connection reference may be made to Article II (b) of the principal agreement, whereby administrations and communication carriers enter into traffic agreements with respect to their use of channels of communication provided by the system, services to public facilities, and divisions of revenue. Reference is also made to Article 10 of the Special Agreement, which relates to contracts placed by COMSAT concerning the space segment.[53]

A more detailed examination of the operation of the two agreements in practice could reveal further difficulties which arise from the dual role of COMSAT. While compromise solutions can no doubt be worked out to reconcile the controlling functions of COMSAT with those of a controlled corporation, there is danger that control may remain purely formal,[54] especially since unequal voting powers of the participating countries tend to reduce international control to limited significance.

At the Annual Meeting of the American Society of International Law in April, 1967, the view was expressed that the structure of INTELSAT could be improved by divorcing the problem of voting powers from the financial aspects of the quota system.[55] Thus the system of weighted voting would be replaced by a regime of equality in voting despite inequality of ownership. The contrary view is that, while in consultative or even regulatory international agencies equality of voting is possible despite inequality of power, operational agencies such as the IMF and IBRD and the International Commodity Councils (particularly the Tin Council), which actually engage in businesslike transactions, have usually adopted the system of weighted voting. Weighted voting reflects more accurately the differences between the contribution of the contracting parties to the common pool and the operations of the agencies. Whatever the outcome of this difference of views, there is no doubt that the quota and voting system should be reexamined during the negotiations, which will lead to the conversion of the interim arrangements into a permanent arrangement.

At the Fifty-second Conference of the International Law Association in Helsinki, Dr. Zhukov, the Soviet representative, made certain significant statements.[56] He recalled that the Soviet Union had put three Molniya communication satellites into orbit and was engaged in building up its own communication satellite system. He emphasized, however, that the existence of more than one system is unfortunate and that efforts should be made to establish a single global system with all countries having equal rights to the use of the spectrum. The single world system should, in his view, be an intergovernmental entity without participation by private bodies. Only states can exercise responsibilities in outer space. If private bodies operate in this field, they should be under the strictest control of their governments. According to Dr. Zhukov, ITU should be entrusted with the preparation of a new basis for such a system and the reorganization of INTELSAT on the above lines should be attempted. The Soviet representative gave the following reasons for the creation of a single system: (1) It would ensure better use of frequencies under ITU control; (2) it would promote an economic and efficient exploitation of the entire spectrum; (3) it would exclude harmful interference more effectively than two or more systems operating side by side; and (4) it would promote the development of means of communication in space, as well as in associated ground networks, while making the most economical use of resources. If one system cannot be established, coordination between two or more systems will be necessary, but the problems of coordination would be complicated. It could be effected directly between the existing systems through ITU as intermediary, or through a special agency to be established. Consultations would have to be resorted to in accordance with the Outer Space Treaty.[57]

It is submitted that neither the second nor the third solution is feasible. ITU is not likely to undertake the role of intermediary between two operational systems. As a "regulatory" agency it is not equipped to do the work. On the other hand, the establishment of a special interoperational agency does not seem to be useful. If agreement is reached between the two systems, their bilateral relationship is not likely to be institutionalized.

Finally, a few observations should be offered regarding the legal character of INTELSAT. The principal agreement does not confer legal personality on the organization. It seems to be a consortium of states or telecommunication entities without separate legal existence, perhaps in the same way as the contracting parties to the General Agreement on Tariffs and Trade (GATT). The principal agreement explains the structure and function of the Committee, the governing body, but it makes no reference to the chief executive officer. The latter could have been a repository of legal powers and his position might be constitutionally defined in the future by permanent arrangements. However, it may be noted that the International Organisation Immunities Act has been extended by the President of the United States to INTELSAT, thus conferring on it and its organs all appropriate privileges and immunities and giving the agency legal status in American municipal law.[58] No conclusions can be drawn from this as to the position of INTELSAT in international law. Such status could become precise under the permanent arrangements if, for instance, INTELSAT were to be given express power to conclude international agreements and treaties which would be evidence of international legal personality.[59]

Although there are no express provisions in the principal agreement directly referring to legal personality, Article 14 of the Special Agreement is indirectly relevant to it. It envisages the establishment of an impartial tribunal which would decide all legal disputes arising in connection with the Special Agreement, affecting the rights and obligations of signatories. The tribunal would make its decisions in accordance with general principles of law.[60] To give effect to these provisions, Article 14 refers to the possible conclusion of a supplementary agreement. In fact, such an agreement came into force on November 21, 1966. It states that the arbitral tribunal to be constituted will be competent to undertake the examination of the constitutionality of action or inaction of the committee.[61] What is essential in the definition of the arbitral procedure is the provision to the effect that the signatories to the Special Agreement, as well as the Committee, can be parties to arbitration. If it is true to say that the arbitral tribunal is an international judicial organ, it is also possible to maintain that the Committee having *locus standi* before the tribunal has a measure of legal status in international law.

The tribunal is constituted by the selection of one member by each party to the dispute. The two members then select the president of the tribunal from a panel of seven legal experts appointed by the Committee. If the two members are unable to reach agreement on the selection of the president, the chairman of the panel will designate him. To this extent, arbitration is compulsory and similar to the arbitration process of UPU except for the fact that the Bureau of UPU also has the right to appoint an arbitrator for the noncooperative respondent. As shown above, ITU and ICAO adopted arbitration provisions similar to those of UPU.[62]

INTELSAT operations are well advanced and they have created a new cooperative reality in outer space. The first of the commercial communications satellites (Early Bird) was launched in 1965. It provides high quality services between North America and Europe. This satellite of a synchronous character [63] was followed by Intelsat II over the Pacific (1967) and another satellite over the Atlantic. Each of the Intelsat II satellites is used in conjunction with standard earth stations and provides almost three times the circuit capacity of the most recent transatlantic cables. Intelsat III satellite (1968) and the satellites planned for 1970–1971 will have an even greater capacity,[64] and they will achieve global coverage.[65]

As mentioned above, the view has been expressed that it is possible to conceive a sort of parking space over the equator reserved for Intelsat synchronous satellites.[66] One may ask whether such reservation creates any rights for the state from whose territory a satellite is launched and whose "nationality" it possesses. A tentative answer was given to this question by John A. Johnson, vice-president of COMSAT, when he said: "It would seem that the first occupier should have the right to continue to occupy a particular orbital location but this situation clearly underlines the necessity for international coordination." [67]

Whatever the merits of this answer (see Chapter I, note 3), it would not imply any right of occupation of outer space or outer space frequencies on whose guidance and operation the life of the satellite depends. Such occupation would be reconcilable neither with the Legal Principles and the Outer Space Treaty nor with ITU practice and United States official views.

While IATA and INTELSAT are quasi-public agencies in the field of global communication and operate on lines similar to those developed by public international organs of communication, and while they constitute an extension of organization and expert diplomacy from the interstate field of cooperation to a wider field with participation of private entities, entities of a purely private nature have appeared in the field of maritime transport. Reference has already been made to International Shipping Conferences which perform, in a decentralized way, functions similar to those of IATA, namely, rate fixing and coordination of services. Moreover, the International Maritime Committee, established in 1898, which was instrumental in promoting the conclusion of a number of international maritime conventions,[68] is a body composed of delegates of national shipping associations.

Finally, Lloyd's Register in London is an independent, noncommercial society not endowed with legal personality. Its main function is the establishment of construction and maintenance standards for ships. Its history goes back to 1760 when a group of marine underwriters formed a committee for issuing a register which recorded details of ships likely to be presented for insurance. In 1834 a general committee composed of shipowners, shipbuilders, and underwriters was founded. It decided on classification (grading) on the advice of surveyors without government interference. The classification certificates of Lloyd's are accepted by all maritime nations, many of whom have established national committees as evidence that the minimum requirements in respect of structural strength have been complied with. The register shows the result of the survey of ships, and it also records all mercantile tonnage whether classified with Lloyd's or not. The recording of tonnage is automatic, and Lloyd's Register accepts the nationality of a vessel as conferred on her by the registering state without going into the genuineness of the link between state and vessel. The problem was taken up by the

International Court of Justice in its Advisory Opinion in the IMCO case relating to the elections to the Maritime Safety Committee.[69]

Although Lloyd's Register is not a governmental or intergovernmental body, it may by delegation perform certifying functions under certain intergovernmental maritime agreements and thus act like a quasi-public agency. Some of the details of these agreements (the Safety of Life at Sea and Load Line Convention) have been discussed above.

THE NATIONALITY OF VEHICLES
OF GLOBAL COMMUNICATION
AND THE TECHNIQUE OF REGISTRATION

《《《〇》》》

It has been emphasized in the Introduction to this inquiry that the international lawyer examining the rules of global communication is confronted with certain basic elements, namely, operational communication space, the vehicles or means of communication, and persons, cargo, and messages which are the object of communication services. After a discussion of the legal status of communication space and its impact on the organization of communication services, problems of standardization of the technical law and of the structure and functions of the agencies of communication were analyzed.

As this inquiry is carried out within the framework of public international law and organization, all problems of municipal law (public and private) relating to vehicles of communication and passengers or cargo are, in principle, beyond its scope. However, vehicles of communication acquire the nationality of one or another state and come permanently within a particular system of law. The process of acquiring nationality and carrying a system of law (on a vehicle) across national boundaries, whenever it operates on international routes, must be the concern of the international lawyer. As nationality is granted to vehicles by national registration and as the prototype of such registration has been established in maritime law and has served as a model in other fields of communication, a brief discussion of the problems connected with the registration of ships will first be attempted.

International lawyers have maintained that the registration technique is peculiar to the law of real property and that its application to ships is inappropriate since ships are movable property.[1] However, ships are movable property *sui generis*.[2] Although registration cannot create new territory and although in the absence of territory the flag state has no territorial jurisdiction over ships,[3] the law of the flag governs persons and events on board ship. Registration establishes a link between a ship and a particular system of municipal law and subjects the ship to a definite legal regime. It removes the danger of lawlessness from a piece of floating property which has the capacity of offering, under its flag, a temporary home to an *ad hoc* community and which thus acquires a quasi-territorial status.[4]

The question may arise whether states enjoy complete autonomy whenever they act as registering entities and introduce their law on board ship or whether there are any limitations upon this autonomy in international law. After offering a brief answer to the question, discussion will be extended to registration of aircraft and the legal regime on board aircraft.

The United States Supreme Court held that states have, under rules of international law, the right to determine the conditions for granting nationality to a merchant vessel. But state practice is far from uniform in this field. Some states require that the owners of ships applying for registration must be nationals of the state of registration, such as the United States, Great Britain, Germany, Japan, and the Soviet Union. Other states do not have strict requirements in this respect.[5] Panama, Liberia, and Honduras are some of the states in this category.[6] As will be seen, those are the states which have registered large numbers of foreign-owned or controlled ships, granting them what is generally called "flags of convenience."

The Geneva Convention on the High Seas (1958) states, in Article 5, that "each state shall fix the conditions for the grant of its nationality to ships, for the registration of ships in its territory, and for the right to fly its flag. Ships have the nationality of the State whose flag they are entitled to fly." This part of Article 5 would indicate that states possess complete autonomy in establishing links between ships and their municipal laws. But the rest of the article qualifies the autonomous regime of registration by requiring the existence of "a genuine link between the State and the ship." In particular the state "must effectively exercise its jurisdiction and control in administrative, technical and social matters over ships flying its flag." [7] There is no reference to the nationality of shipowners in Article 5.

As stated above, Lloyd's Register is *inter alia* concerned with the recording (registration) of registered tonnage. Registration in Lloyd's Register does not reflect the genuineness or nongenuineness of the link between the registering state and ships, but it indicates, in appropriate order, all shipowning [8] nations of the world. It may be stated that the extent of shipowning may have legal consequences for those states which by order of priority enjoy rights as "the largest shipowning nations." In this connection the Advisory Opinion of the International Court of Justice in the IMCO case should be discussed. In this case the court dealt with the elections to one of IMCO's organs, the Maritime Safety Committee. The court's opinion is indirectly relevant to the problem of the "genuine link."

According to Article 28 of the IMCO Convention [9] (original text) "the Maritime Safety Committee shall consist of 14 [now 16] members elected by the Assembly from the members, governments of these nations having an important interest in maritime safety, of which not less than eight shall be the largest shipowning nations." Here shipowning indicates registration, not ownership. The remaining members of the Committee are elected so as to ensure adequate representation of other nations "with an important interest in maritime safety, such as nations interested in the supply of large numbers of crews or in the carriage of large numbers of berthed and unberthed passengers, and of major geographical areas."

When the first elections to the Maritime Safety Committee were held, the following eight member states were elected as the eight largest shipowning nations: the United States, United Kingdom, Norway, Japan, Italy, the Netherlands, France, and West Germany. The six elected countries were: Argentina, Canada, Greece, Pakistan, the Soviet Union, and the United Arab Republic. Liberia and Panama complained that they were not elected as part of the group of the eight largest shipowning nations in spite of being registered in Lloyd's Register among the eight nations having the largest tonnage. According to Lloyd's Register this group comprised at the time: the United States, United Kingdom, Liberia, Norway, Japan, Italy, the Netherlands, and Panama. It did not include France and West Germany. Liberia submitted a draft resolution to the IMCO Assembly requesting an Advisory Opinion from the International Court of Justice on the question of the validity of the elections. The question ultimately put to the Court reads as follows: "Is the Maritime Safety Committee of IMCO, which was elected on January 15, 1959, constituted in accordance with the Convention for the establishment of the Organisation?"

The Court gave its Advisory Opinion on June 8, 1960, nine votes to five. Its answer to the question set out above was that the Maritime Safety Committee was not constituted in accordance with the IMCO Convention. One of the questions raised in the proceedings was that of the genuine link between Liberia and Panama (as ship-registering countries) on the one hand, and the foreign-owned or controlled ships registered by them on the other. It was alleged that most of the tonnage registered in Liberia and Panama had no connection with the two countries. The majority of the judges relied on evidence obtained from Lloyd's Register without reference to the problem of the genuine link and the nature of Liberia and Panama's ownership.[10]

Some of the countries defending the validity of the elections pointed to the Geneva Convention on the High Seas (1958), which embodied the principle of the genuine link in Article 5.[11] It was also pointed out that only countries having an important interest in maritime safety, as defined or at least indicated in Article 28, could be elected to the Maritime Safety Committee and that Liberia and Panama, despite their registered tonnage,[12] were not in this category of maritime powers. Moreover, it was argued that the word "elect" in Article 28 gave the Assembly power to chose between candidate states in the election. Elections were not automatic. It was alleged that a candidate state had to satisfy the electors, that it had an important interest in maritime safety, and that this applied to all candidates including the eight largest ship-owning nations.[13]

Liberia replied that Article 28(c) had a mandatory character, and thus the Assembly had no alternative but to rely on Lloyd's Register as indicating conclusively the eight largest shipowning nations. The law of registration was supreme and the eight countries at the head of the list of the numbers of registered vessels must be presumed to have an important interest in maritime safety. Panama also objected to the elections to the Maritime Safety Committee on the ground that they went "behind the flag," which constituted a violation of sovereignty. As stated above, the court considered the elections invalid. It expressed the opinion that interest in maritime safety of the eight largest shipowning countries as determined on the basis of Lloyd's Register must be considered as "axiomatic."

Critics of the Advisory Opinion [14] have argued that registration may be conclusive evidence of the national character of a vessel but that its evidential value for the purpose of ascertaining a state's important interest in maritime safety is questionable. They also point out that Article 28 speaks about the election of the Maritime Safety Committee by the Assembly and that election cannot be made mandatory by reference to a statistical criterion such as figures in Lloyd's Register.[15] The Advisory Opinion by implication accepts the validity of flags of convenience, at least for the purpose of Article 28 of the IMCO Convention. We are thus left with an unsolved issue, for the irrelevancy of the genuine link for purposes of the above article does not mean that the genuine link as defined in Article 5 of the Geneva Convention on the High Seas is irrelevant for all other purposes. Otherwise its inclusion in Article 5 could not be considered as meaningful.

The concept of the genuine link has also appeared in the field of international civil aviation. A survey of bilateral air transport agreements shows that they contain *inter alia* the substantial ownership and effective control clause (apart from the fair and equal opportunity clause discussed above). The clause gives a contracting party the right to withhold or revoke rights to operate an air service in its airspace or on its territory if the party is not satisfied that the substantial ownership and effective control of the designated airline of the other contracting state is vested in that State or in its nationals.[16] There is no restriction on the nationality of aircraft used by the particular airline.[17]

What matters then is the genuine link between an airline and the country in which it is incorporated. If the other contracting party is satisfied that such a link exists, permission to operate should be granted and respected during the period of its stipulated validity.[18] The airline can employ aircraft registered in another country and the foreign nationality of aircraft is no cause for withholding permission to operate or for revoking it.[19]

As to the nationality of aircraft, the Chicago Convention of 1944 states in Article 17 that "aircraft have the nationality of the State in which they are registered," and Article 19 gives the state of registration complete autonomy as to conditions of registration. It states that registration "shall be made in accordance with its laws and regulations." [20] It is suggested that these provisions are declaratory of international customary law.

Attention had been drawn in the Introduction to Article 77 of the Chicago Convention, which authorizes the ICAO Council to determine "in which manner the provisions of the Convention relating to the nationality of aircraft shall apply to aircraft operated by international operating agencies." The question arises whether the ICAO Council has the power to authorize international registration of aircraft waiving the requirements of registration in a particular state. If so, do such aircraft have the rights and privileges of aircraft which are registered in such a state and have its nationality?

The view has been expressed that the provisions of the Chicago Convention are not an obstacle to joint international registration and that the determination of the Council has sufficient effect for international registration to be recognized by other contracting states.[21] However, even if the ICAO Council would admit the possibility of international registration, that would be far from bringing about a fundamental change in world civil aviation, for such registration would only apply to joint operating organizations of a limited regional character.[22]

If a summary of legal trends in the field of nationality of vehicles of world communication were attempted, it would be fair to say that states have successfully asserted their complete autonomy of conferring nationality on aircraft. The concept of the genuine link has appeared only in relation to airlines in bilateral air transport agreements, possibly as a concession to those systems of municipal law which insist on respect for such a link. In the field of shipping the concept was adopted by the Geneva Convention on the High Seas (1958) but suffered a setback in the IMCO case when the International Court of Justice gave its

Advisory Opinion without referring to the concept of the genuine link. Generally speaking, the emancipation of nationality of ship and aircraft from the requirements of the genuine link, much as it may be dictated by financial reasons, tends to strengthen the idea of what may be called "nationality by free choice." World communication services as a whole may benefit from such flexibility of the law, for the possibility of shifting ships and aircraft of one nationality to communication enterprises in countries of another nationality may help to distribute the technical resources of global communication on an international scale and thus to promote an expansion of services to the benefit of the general public all over the world.

It may be relevant at this point to draw attention to a number of conventions concluded in the field of private international air law. It has been mentioned that they are outside the scope of this inquiry,[23] but at least one of them, the Tokyo Convention, is of importance for the legal regime on board aircraft, and indirectly for its legal status. Before a summary discussion of this convention is attempted, a few general observations relating to the legal regime on board ship, aircraft, and satellite may be offered.

Registration results in the establishment of the law of the flag on board ship. But as stated earlier, the jurisdiction of the flag state is not territorial, although a number of international lawyers applied the fiction of territoriality to ships. Whatever the correctness of this view, the flag state is competent to deal with all matters of criminal and civil law which originate on the ship. This is the situation with respect to events which take place on the high seas.[24]

As to ships exercising the right of innocent passage through territorial waters, Article 17 of the Geneva Convention on the Territorial Sea and the Contiguous Zone (1958) requires such ships to "comply with the laws and regulations enacted by the coastal State in conformity with [the articles of the Convention] and other rules of international law and, in particular, with such laws and regulations relating to transport and navigation." In the last part of the article, emphasis is put on the external legal regime relating to a ship in innocent passage, which must obey the local rules of navigation. As to a ship's internal legal regime, namely, the law in force on board ship, Article 19 states that criminal jurisdiction of the coastal state should not be exercised on board a foreign ship passing through the territorial sea unless the consequences of the crime are external, that is, unless they extend to the coastal state, or disturb the peace of the country or the good order of the territorial sea.[25] Article 20 also excludes the exercise of civil jurisdiction by the coastal state in relation to a ship in innocent passage. If the ship is in a foreign harbor, similar provisions would apply. In cases of conflict of jurisdiction the law of the coastal state will prevail over the law of the flag whenever the effects of events on board ship are external and affect the legal regime of the coastal state.[26]

Aircraft and satellites, like ships, are linked to a system of municipal law by registration. Although they follow the overall pattern of maritime law, it is difficult to speak without reservation about the law of the flag of an aircraft or satellite. The concept of "fictional territory" is not applicable to them either.

As to the legal regime on board aircraft, it has not been possible to secure uniformity of approach to the problem by member states of the family of nations. Section 7 of the American Uniform Aeronautics Act of 1922, adopted by more than twenty American states, applies the law of the territorial state to aircraft. The English legal system has not accepted the law of registration as the primary law in the legal regime on board aircraft.[27]

The question came up for consideration in two cases, *R. v. Martin* [28] and *R. v. Naylor*.[29] The facts of the first case showed that the accused were arraigned on an indictment which alleged that they committed offenses against the Dangerous Drugs Act of 1951 and the Dangerous Drugs Regulations of 1953. They were members of the crew of a British aircraft, and it was found that they had carried opium from Bahrein to Singapore. This was an offense against Regulation 3, which states that "a person shall not be in possession of a drug unless he is generally so authorised. . . ." It was conceded that the regulation applied only to acts committed in England, that is, unauthorized possession of dangerous drugs in England, but the prosecution argued that Section 62(1) of the Civil Aviation Act of 1949 converted such acts into offenses if committed on board British aircraft. The judge rejected this argument and considered the offense of unauthorized possession of drugs as one of domestic application only. Thus he refused to apply English law, which was the law of registration of the aircraft. He said he would apply English law as an exception to the rule in the case of universal offenses, as distinguished from offenses of domestic application, such as murder or theft.

In *R. v. Naylor* the judge was faced with the offense of theft [30] committed by a passenger on board a British aircraft over the high seas. Unlike the judge in *R. v. Martin,* the judge in this case expressed the view that "any act or omission which would constitute an offence done in England is made an offence if made on board a British aircraft." Thus we must assume that the judge allowed Section 62(1) to extend English penal law, as the law of registration of the aircraft,[31] to persons and events on British aircraft. He qualified this rule by stating that if an offense is "one of domestic application" as it was in *R. v. Martin,* then Section 62(1) would not have the above effect.

In spite of the difference between the two cases,[32] the decisions in both are based on the assumption that British aircraft are neither an area of domestic application of the law of registration nor an extension of British territory in any fictional way. The conclusions reached by judicial authority are hardly satisfactory, particularly because of danger of partial lawlessness on board aircraft.[33] Consequently an attempt was made at the Tokyo Conference in 1963 to pass a convention aiming at legal uniformity in this filed.

The convention [34] accords prima facie a prominent position, in respect of trial and punishment of offenses committed on board aircraft, to the state of registration. Whether this will ultimately lead to the effective establishment of the law of registration (nationality) as the governing law is more than doubtful. According to Article 3(1): "the State of registration of the aircraft is competent to exercise jurisdiction over offences and acts committed on board (aircraft). . . ." Consequently, Article 3(2) imposes an *obligation* on any contracting state which is a state of registration of an aircraft to "take such measures as may be necessary to establish its jurisdiction" over offenses committed on board aircraft registered in such a state. However, Article 4 states a number of exceptions to the (primary) jurisdiction of the state of registration which tend to whittle down its validity.[35]

Specifically, the following states, apart from the state of registration, may interfere with an aircraft in flight in order to exercise criminal jurisdiction over an offense committed on board aircraft: (1) the state in whose territory the offense has effect; (2) the state whose national or permanent resident has committed the offense or against whose national or permanent resident it has been committed; (3) the state against whose security the offense is directed; (4) the state whose rules or regulations relating to flight or maneuver of aircraft have been violated by the aircraft; [36] (5) the state which finds it necessary to exercise its jurisdiction to ensure the observance of any obligation under a multilateral international agreement. Reading these exceptions it is difficult to escape from the impression that in a number of cases the law of the territorial state [37] would successfully compete with the law of the state of registration. The jurisdiction of the state of registration would, subject to reservations, prevail in the case of offenses committed on board aircraft over the high seas or over territory not subject to sovereignty.

As to the municipal laws of various countries, the principle of territoriality is given preference in the common law countries while the civil law countries generally apply the nationality principle. In the Tokyo Convention, a compromise solution has been attempted. The contracting states agreed on the concurrent jurisdiction of the state of registration (primary jurisdiction) and of other states (Article 4).[38] Reference may be made to Article 16(1) of the convention relating to extradition, which treats offenses committed on board aircraft registered in a contracting state as if they had been committed not only in the place in which they have occurred but also in the territory of the Registry State. The application of this provision for purposes of extradition would point to the quasi-territorial nature of the interior of the aircraft. However, Article 16(2) makes it clear that "nothing in this Convention shall be deemed to create an obligation to grant extradition," which destroys the general policy pursued by the drafters of the convention to avoid lawlessness in the case of offenses committed on board aircraft, particularly when the state of the presence of the offender does not assume jurisdiction and it is impossible to bring him before any competent judicial authority. A duty of assuming jurisdiction would only arise if the offender disembarked in the state of registration (Article 3). Otherwise, the states enumerated in Article 4 are authorized to assume alternative jurisdiction and may or may not do so.[39]

This brief discussion of the Tokyo Convention is not intended to give a complete picture of its provisions, but it may help in understanding the controversial problems relating to the consequences of registration (conferment of nationality) for the legal regime prevailing on board aircraft and for its legal status.

The situation with regard to satellites seems to be different from that of aircraft. It is difficult to see any reason why the law of registration or the law of the launching state [40] should not normally apply to the legal regime on board satellites. Satellites do not travel to areas under foreign sovereignty. They tend to return to the territory from which they were launched, or they terminate their travel in the high seas. Apart from unforeseen circumstances when a satellite may be out of control, its main operational area is the outer space, which is under no state's sovereignty. The route from the launching site and return to the national state would hardly affect other states except when the satellite passes fleetingly through some foreign airspace. Thus the legal regime on board satellites is bound to be governed during its lifetime by the law of registration (nationality) as determined by the Outer Space treaty and practice.[41] Unlike the case of aircraft, territorial law would not compete with the law of registration in outer space. It is questionable whether any territorial law could be relevant to a satellite. If so, the fiction of exoterritoriality could be applied to satellites as they are within the sphere of orbital forces and as the law applicable to events on board outer space vehicles is not geocentric and need not gravitate toward any territorial legal system.[42] The law of registration (nationality) which the satellite takes with itself into the exoatmospheric region can well govern persons and events inside its confines.[43]

LEGAL FACTORS SUPPORTING
THE GLOBALITY OF AGENCIES
OF INTERNATIONAL COMMUNICATION

《《《〇》》》

Globality has been found to be a common factor of the agencies of communication discussed here. As stated earlier, the law of global communication dates back to the first establishment of oceanic routes in the sixteenth and seventeenth centuries. It was part and parcel of the classical law of nations which, following the natural law concept, became a universal legal system and applied to all nations irrespective of continent, race, and civilization. It promoted universal intercourse in response to a social reality extending to the whole world. The process of world integration gathered momentum in the eighteenth and nineteenth centuries and the institutionalization of postal and telecommunication services was followed by similar developments in the fields of radiocommunication and civil aviation. A number of factors of legal significance which tended to support the universality of these agencies and to remove some of the obstacles to the global adherence of states deserve attention.

UPU and ITU were, up to their incorporation into the family of the Specialized Agencies of the United Nations, "open unions" (*unions ouvertes*), that is, agencies to which any sovereign country could accede by a unilateral declaration.[1] A country acceding to UPU simply notified the Swiss government of its adherence to the convention. Similar provisions applied to ITU and they were instrumental in raising membership of these unions to the level of globality.

The situation changed after World War II. At present only members of the United Nations may accede unilaterally to UPU (Article 11,1 of the Vienna Constitution). Nonmembers of the United Nations must apply to UPU for admission, and the application requires the approval of at least two-thirds of the member countries of UPU (Article 11,4). According to the final protocol to the Constitution, countries that were members of UPU prior to the entry of the Constitution into force on January 1, 1966, but that had not signed the Constitution, may accede to it at any time by depositing an instrument of accession with the Swiss government. South Africa and Kenya acceded in this way to the Acts of the Union.[2]

Membership of ITU extends, according to Article 1 of the Montreux Convention, to countries listed in Annex 1 and to countries (members of the United Nations) not listed in the Annex which accede unilaterally to ITU. But countries which are not members of the United Nations must be admitted by a vote of two-thirds of the members. On the other hand, the convention introduced associate membership (Article 1), which allows partially sovereign entities, including trust territories, to participate in the work of the organization, though without the right to vote. UPU had earlier admitted partially sovereign entities to membership, and according to Article 2 of the Vienna Constitution, the term "member country" extends to certain groups of countries such as the United States territories, including the Pacific Islands under trusteeship, the Spanish territories in Africa, the overseas French territories, the overseas British territories, the Dutch Antilles and Surinam, the Portuguese provinces of West Africa, and the Portuguese provinces of East Africa and Oceania. The separate representation of these entities in UPU and of associate members in ITU results either in plural voting exercised by some of the European powers and the United States or their increased influence with the agencies (ITU).

The link of ICAO with the United Nations is even more pronounced than that of UPU and ITU. Members of the United Nations can unilaterally adhere to ICAO and so can states associated with them and states which remained neutral during the last war (Article 92). But according to Article 93, states other than the original signatories of the Chicago Convention and those indicated in Article 92 require a four-fifths vote of the Assembly for admission to ICAO. The Assembly may prescribe further conditions of admission and in each case "the assent of any State invaded or attacked during the (last) war by the State seeking admission shall be necessary." In practice this provision tended to lose its original significance.[3]

With respect to IMCO, Article 6 of the convention relates to admission of United Nations members, by signature and/or acceptance, and to nonmembers of the United Nations invited to the UN Maritime Conference in 1948 (Article 7). Other states require a vote of two-thirds for admission (Article 8). Article 9 introduced associate membership. Associate members participate in the work of the organization but cannot vote and are not eligible for membership in certain organs of IMCO. Article 11 declares that "no State or Territory may become or remain a Member of the Organisation contrary to a resolution of the General Assembly of the United Nations." Thus in all agencies of global communication UN politics affected the membership system in various forms following their affiliation with the United Nations.[4] Such affiliation had been originally resisted by some of these agencies.

Certain nonmember states such as East Germany, North Korea, North Vietnam, and the government of the mainland of China (Peking), not being able to participate in the world network of postal and telecommunication services, maintain relations with the network through bilateral agreements concluded with members of UPU and ITU (see Article 4 of the Vienna Constitution), and they have informal access to UPU documentation.[5]

A characteristic feature of the UPU regime is the existence of certain internal customary rules which have contributed to its universality. These rules apply in cases when states which sign the convention or other acts of UPU are unable to ratify or approve them. It will be recalled that the UPU Acts have been reclassified by the Vienna Congress (Article 22 of the Constitution). They consist of the Constitution, the General Regulations, the UPU Convention and its Regulations, and the Special Arrangements accompanied by their own Regulations. The Regulations of the Convention and of the Special Agreements have been adopted by postal administrations. Other acts are dealt with by plenipotentiaries of governments. Only the Constitution requires ratification. The other acts are simply approved by member states or postal administrations.

Ratification must take place "as soon as possible" (Article 25), which in practice means not later than three years after the coming into force of the Constitution.[6] However, in the past nonratification by a state within this period did not necessarily mean withdrawal from the organization. A nonratifying member state which continued to observe the provisions of UPU Acts and complied with the UPU regime was presumed to have ratified it tacitly. Such presumed continuous adherence to the organization allowed UPU to preserve its universality. Large numbers of countries have failed at various times to ratify in time the acts of UPU and some countries have never ratified them. But they have always complied with the provisions of a new convention and observed them in practice. It has been customary for other member countries which had ratified the convention to treat the nonratifying countries as participants in the UPU regime.

This custom must still be considered valid, not only in case of revision of the Constitution but also in case of approval of other acts. It would be possible to speak today about presumed, implied, or tacit approval of these acts (except the Constitution) in the same way as it was customary to respect presumed, implied, or tacit ratification.[7]

Similar precedents or even usages have appeared in ITU practice. The Telegraph Union and the Radiotelegraph Union had permitted countries which, in the absence of ratification, had not acquired formal membership to participate in conferences. When the Radio, Telegraph, and Telephone Conferences were held in 1938, about twenty countries which were legally not contracting parties to the ITU Convention were allowed to participate in the meetings. This group of countries included nine Latin American republics and some European countries such as France, Greece, Portugal, and Rumania. It was argued that the Telecommunication Conference was a plenipotentiary body endowed with the supreme powers of the union, and it could therefore admit any country to participation irrespective of noncompliance with some of the provisions of the ITU Convention.[8]

It follows from this brief survey of certain provisions of the constituent texts of the agencies of global communication, as well as of extratreaty rules relevant to membership in these agencies, that some of them were instrumental in removing the obstacles to universal membership. The conversion of these organizations into Specialized Agencies of the United Nations was not a constructive factor from the technical point of view. But by that time UPU and ITU had already reached the goal of universality, and thus United Nations political influence was not detrimental to the maintenance of global technical networks of communication. The existing universality of UPU and ITU is protected by the absence of expulsion and suspension provisions in their constituent texts.[9] However, suspension provisions are included in Articles 62 and 93 bis of the ICAO Convention and in Article 42 of the IMCO Convention. Article 11 of the IMCO Convention states that "no State or Territory may become or remain a Member of the Organisation contrary to a resolution of the General Assembly of the United Nations," which implies automatic termination of membership in IMCO in case of expulsion from the United Nations.

Apart from express provisions in treaties or rules established in other ways, there are further developments within some of the agencies of global communication which have been instrumental in preserving universal membership. It was shown that CINA had introduced a legislative process for the amendment of technical Annexes and that a number of powers were unable to join the Commission because of their reluctance to submit to international legislation in the strict sense of the word. It is for this reason, *inter alia,* that ICAO converted the legislative process relating to technical standards into a quasi-legislative procedure which makes it possible for all states to join the organization. The USSR was not a member until 1970, but it was integrated into the process of technical standardization through bilateral transport agreements with some of the members of ICAO, such as the United States and the United Kingdom.

Emphasis has been put on the universality of the agencies of world communication, because it is a basic condition for the proper functioning of mechanisms and services which cannot be split into smaller networks, except by a measure of decentralization of the global unit. It has been shown that political considerations tend to prevent the achievement of absolute universality. Nonadmission to the United Nations entails exclusion from the Specialized Agencies. In certain cases this sort of penalty may be justified by overriding considerations of power politics. In the field of global communication it seems less expedient. Nonparticipating entities are integrated into the existing networks of communication through the backdoor, through bilateral links with member states, and by informal media for maintaining liaison. There has been controversy whether a universal agency has legal personality in international law vis-à-vis nonmember states (*erga omnes*).

The International Court of Justice in its Advisory Opinion in the Reparation of Injuries case [10] declared that "the vast majority of the members of the international community had the power, in conformity with international law, to bring into being an entity possessing objective international personality, and not merely personality recognised by them alone" (nonobjective international personality). This statement applies to the United Nations, which count among its members the vast majority of powers. It applies equally to the Specialized Agencies of the United Nations including the agencies of global communication. Objective international personality is therefore one of the legal attributes of UPU, ITU, IMCO, and ICAO.

SUMMARY AND CONCLUSIONS

《《《》》

Problems relating to global communication fall broadly into two categories, those pertaining to the field of technical regulation, and those dealing with the organization of services from the commercial point of view.
There is an intimate connection between the two, for progress or obstruction in one field will have constructive or detrimental effects in the
other. In all branches of global communication, agreement has been
reached on the uniformity of the technical law. On the other hand, competition between member states of the family of nations and their sover-
eign-mindedness have been retarding factors in the commercial organization of transport services. Sovereignty is the determining element in
the definition of the legal status of the space in which global communication services operate. Therefore, the present inquiry started with a
discussion of the various operational areas of communication, the high
seas, the airspace, outer space, and radio space, and the impact of
their legal status in international law on world communication services.

Attention has been drawn to the paradoxical fact that the oldest
branch of global communication, maritime transport, was the last to be
institutionalized (IMCO). Intergovernmental agreement in this field was
for centuries superfluous in view of the freedom of the high sea—a
principle firmly established in international customary law, as well as
embodied in treaty (Geneva Convention in 1958). The organization of
maritime services was left largely to private initiative, and private agencies took not only the responsibility for the promotion of maritime con-

ventions and safety regulations but also for the coordination of national shipping policies, including rate fixing. In this respect reference was made to the activities of international shipping conferences, the International Maritime Committee, and Lloyd's Register.

There are, however, a number of counteracting factors which make it increasingly difficult for the community of nations to reap all the benefits of the freedom of the sea. First of all, the entry of merchant vessels into foreign harbors has not become a right in international law. Apart from exceptional cases such as distress, the receiving state tends to allow foreign vessels to enter its harbors and to load and unload goods and embark and disembark passengers as a matter of *usage* only. There has been no *opinio juris* to convert this usage into an international obligation with a corresponding right of entry. The arbitral tribunal in the Aramco Oil Company case, relying on the Geneva Convention of 1923, held in favor of the existence of such *opinio juris*. However, freedom of entry of merchant vessels into foreign harbors, as stipulated in the convention, is hardly declaratory of international customary law since the Geneva Convention of 1923 has not secured universal adherence. States tend to fall back on bilateral solutions which create a vast network of treaties without the advantage of a multilateral and global solution. Moreover, government policies supporting their own national maritime interests by subsidies, flag discrimination, and other restrictive measures tend to reduce further the benefits which the family of nations is entitled to expect from freedom of ocean navigation as it has existed since the days of Grotius. IMCO has been authorized to deal with matters of discriminatory or restrictive practices but the fact that it is not prepared or allowed to intervene in practice, except at the risk of jeopardizing its technical activities, has been discouraging. The situation is still further aggravated by the growing claims of states over the continental shelf, which extend to distances that are bound to affect the freedom of maritime navigation.[1]

Civil aviation had a different start from that of maritime transport. It is the only branch of global communication in which the legal status of the operational area of communication (airspace) was subordinated to the requirements of national sovereignty from the very beginning. It may be understandable that states insisted on sovereignty in airspace for strategic and commercial reasons, but it must be considered an unfortunate lack of foresight that such sovereignty was defined in the CINA Convention of 1919 and in the Chicago Convention of 1944 as "complete and exclusive." The adoption by states of such an extreme attitude confined the whole of civil aviation to a network of bilateral transport agreements regulating scheduled services. While the concept of freedom of passage through foreign airspace was accepted for nonscheduled international flights (Article 5 of the Chicago Convention), sovereignty became a bargaining factor in bilateral negotiations between states for the exchange of rights relating to scheduled services. Of the two agreements concluded apart from the Chicago Convention of 1944, and relating to scheduled services, only the Two Freedom Agreement secured a sufficient number of ratifications to become operative on a wider scale. The Five Freedom Agreement remained largely unratified, and without wide ratification scheduled air services cannot be promoted to the multilateral (global) level which would best ensure their world-wide coordination and proper expansion.

There are, however, certain factors which tend to operate in the direction opposite to that prevailing in maritime communication. Among these factors some appear from within the regime of civil aviation and some from without. Among the first, an initial measure of standardization of the bilateral transport agreement deserves attention. In this respect the Bermuda model has brought about a situation which can be described as cryptomultilateral. A characteristic feature of this type of bilateral agreement is the "fair and equal opportunity" clause, whose objective is a suitable division of traffic all over the world on lines of controlled competition with a consolidating effect within the existing network of bilateral transport agreements. The clause susperseded the pre-Bermuda method of predetermined division of traffic which suffered from lack of flexibility and tended to stifle the expansion of services which depends on a measure of competition.

Another countervailing factor is the incompatibility of the requirements of world traffic control with the division of world airspace according to national frontiers. Each state, being the master of its own airspace, finds itself endowed with sovereignty not for its own sake, in the sense of a proprietary right, but for carrying out its responsibilities for any air services operating above its territory. The collective responsibility of all States for the safety and efficiency of world civil aviation, whatever the nationality of the operating airline or aircraft, is a reality which no state can escape if it wishes to secure the support of other states for its own activities in the field of civil aviation. Annex 11:2,7 of the Chicago Convention recommends a delineation of world airspace for purposes of air traffic services related to the nature of the route structure and the need for efficient service rather than to national boundaries. Thus, sovereignty in airspace tends to be of a *functional* nature and not a concept of "complete and exclusive" validity. Functionalism reveals itself also in the organization of search and rescue services and in accident inquiry.

It is also doubtful whether it is possible to distinguish scheduled from nonscheduled air services with sufficient precision. Specifically, certain services which are formally of a nonscheduled character, for example, some chartered flights, may sometimes carry out cryptoscheduled services and still enjoy the benefits of Article 5 of the Chicago Convention (freedom of passage).

While the above countervailing factors appeared from within the existing bilateral air transport regime, there is also an important factor operating from without the regime, namely, the impossibility of horizontally drawing a distinct boundary between airspace and outer space. The latter is an interest-sharing area in international customary law, as well as in treaty law (*res communis*), and thus the ancient concept of sovereignty above the territory of a state *usque ad coelum* was bound to break down. It must be recalled that the atmosphere, which is the operational area of air navigation and which provides the aerodynamic lift for aircraft, revolves with the earth, thus making it possible to consider a portion of the airspace as an extension and integral part of the subjacent territory. However, where the aerodynamic lift terminates and where orbital forces start operating, no further extension of sovereignty is possible in a definable and static way. The legal status of outer space is not geocentric. Any point in outer space may at any moment be over one country and in the next moment over another. As the boundary between airspace and outer space cannot be drawn with accuracy, the upper region of airspace cannot obey the principle of state sovereignty.

While sovereignty in airspace had a decisive impact on the organization of scheduled air services which were left to bilateral relations, IATA has set up a multilateral machinery of interline operations, rate fixing, and clearing. It maintains uniform fares in the same way as ICAO maintains uniform technical standards. The factors counteracting the consequences of complete and exclusive rights of states in the airspace led to a pluralistic system of mechanisms which tends to modify the absolute character of sovereignty,[2] and to cement the decentralized network of bilateral transport agreements, whether by standardizing the technical law or by coordinating the commercial network of airlines (IATA).

Sovereignty in airspace threatened to become the starting point for defining the legal status of the operational area of radiocommunication. A number of international lawyers, ignoring the facts of science, considered radio frequencies as moving in airspace and thus subject to considerations of national sovereignty. This concept proved untenable and radiocommunication escaped being subject to a regime similar to that of airspace. While the ITU Convention refers to the undefined concept of radio space and while it is possible to conceive of radio space as *res communis* in the sense of an interest-sharing area, it is in a real sense fictional as it lacks the characteristics of a physical area.

Frequencies (radio energy) are within the realm of electromagnetic processes and the question arises whether it is possible to establish a legal title in them. A protracted controversy between the United States and the Soviet Union showed that the vast majority of member countries of ITU rejected the idea of any legal title in frequencies. Neither is it possible to apply to them the rule *prior tempore potior jure*. Instead ITU established administrative machinery with the International Frequency Registration Board in its charge, which performs the functions of an international public trust and sees to the maintenance of public order in the spectrum. The medium for carrying out this function is a planned administrative system of allocation of frequency bands to various services and the registration of individual frequencies assigned by states to radio stations in their territory. Such assignments are notified by states to the IFRB and are subject to an administrative inquiry.

The supreme task of the IFRB is to prevent harmful interference between frequencies in operation. Frequencies which conform to the law of the ITU receive international recognition and protection. Although such protection is only confined to the process of registration and not enforceable by ITU, it has nevertheless proved to be effective, since states must treat the whole system as self-mandatory, with the exception of high frequency broadcasting, which is not within the regime of international protection. The only alternative to its successful operation is chaos in the spectrum and the breakdown of services of safety (maritime and civil aviation), public correspondence, and other essential (fixed) services. No civilized country can afford to provoke or to tolerate the possibility of chaos. International customary law tends to support this solution by prohibiting states to abuse their rights relating to radiocommunication.

The maintenance of spectrum order is of fundamental importance to any space activity—which is inconceivable without radiocommunication. Since outer space and radio space are both beyond the reach of sovereignty, the first following the rules laid down in the Declaration of Legal Principles and the Outer Space Treaty of 1966, it is essential to fit the operation of outer space radiocommunication into the protective mechanism of the IFRB. ITU, which has already allocated frequency bands to space services (Geneva Conference of 1963), is aiming at the necessary coordination in the near future.

The discussion of the legal status of operational areas of global communication need not be extended to world postal services, which operate on land, in the air, and on the seas. However, UPU Conventions, including the Vienna Constitution of 1964, have adopted, in the last ninety years, the concept of a single (world) postal territory which deserves attention. The concept is prima facie symbolic, but it has acquired some territorial meaning thanks to the adoption of the freedom of transit of mail by UPU Conventions. Otherwise the global postal territory is the expression of complete uniformity of municipal postal laws in member countries and of their nondiscriminatory application. Some of the world postal standards generated by UPU are of an extratreaty nature, such as the principle of secrecy and inviolability of correspondence, and the principle of balance of interest of addressor and addressee.

The above discussion has shown the limitations of sovereignty in the organization of communication services. Where the concept of sovereignty was initially applied with complete and exclusive validity resulting in a bilateral regime of services (airspace), it gradually tended to yield to the inherent nature of these services which could not be organized on a global scale through bilateral channels only. Bartering in relation to services is as futile as it is in respect of world trade, and even the most sovereign-minded governments are ultimately driven into multilateralism if they wish to respond to the social reality of world interdependence. Multilateralism on a global scale crept into the network of air transport arrangements through the back door, particularly by interairline agreements (IATA). Moreover, the global allocation of scheduled air services was made possible by reliance on the "fair and equal opportunity" formula which proved flexible and combined the benefits of competition with those of international control.

In other areas of global communication the allocation of services is not obstructed by considerations of sovereignty. The danger of operating services in an interest-sharing area is anarchy. In the field of radiocommunication this is avoided by allocation of frequency bands to various services and by international control of individual frequency assignments. In maritime transport intergovernmental action may be needed to avoid the loss of advantages derived from the freedom of the sea. IMCO is, in principle, empowered to find the remedies but has abstained from intervention. The efficient operation of world postal services, which is not hampered by competition, depends solely on the uniformity of municipal postal laws and regulations and on freedom of transit constitutionally guaranteed and supported by sanctions. The same applies to telecommunication by wire. Submarine cable services rely on treaties and on the freedom of the sea as guaranteed in Article 2(3) of the 1958 Convention on the High Seas.

The next question discussed at some length in this inquiry has been the nature of the technical law of global communication, of the processes of its generation, and of some of the characteristic procedures contained in it.

The first technical law of global communication is to be found in the original UPU and ITU Conventions and Regulations. The conventions were double-purpose instruments containing constitutional or structural as well as technical provisions, and they were periodically renewable. At first the technical law followed the normal processes of treaty law and its revision or amendment were subject to ratification. But in course of time it deviated from this practice in several respects. First, it tended to accumulate predominantly in the special technical texts (Regulations) outside the convention. In the case of the UPU the constitutional split occurred in 1964 when the Vienna Congress placed all constitutional provisions in the permanent (not renewable) Constitution, while leaving the technical law to the convention and to various regulations. While the Constitution requires ratification, the technical law is only subject to approval by member states. The position is the same under the Tokyo Acts (1969), which amended to some extent the Vienna Acts.

The ITU Convention still remains a double-purpose instrument, but the technical Regulations (telegraph, telephone, and radio), which constitute a separate body, contain the bulk of the technical law. Ratification of the convention involves the acceptance of the Regulations (Article 15 of the Montreux Convention). The ICAO Convention is a double-purpose instrument but again the bulk of the technical law is in the Annexes to the convention. The IMCO Convention is a single purpose text, and the whole body of the technical law is in different conventions which are entirely separate from the IMCO Convention.

Progress in the field of communication calls for a prompt regulatory response to technical change. Such response, aimed at uniformity of standards of communication, is provided by the various agencies in different ways. Generally speaking, UPU and ITU have not deviated from traditional treaty processes. The revision or amendment of the technical law is carried out in the same way as the revision or amendment of the constituent instrument of the organization. Decisions are taken by a majority of votes, simple or qualified, but they come into force only for those members which ratify or approve them. They are not binding on the nonratifying (nonapproving) members. The only exception to the above principle is the interval procedure of UPU. Certain decisions adopted in the inter-Congress periods by a majority of votes (simple or qualified) do not require ratification or approval. However, these decisions are adopted multilaterally by contracting in, and thus the process of their adoption is not strictly speaking of a legislative character.

On the other hand, the technical law of CINA, ICAO's predecessor, which was created by the Paris Convention of 1919, was amended by a genuinely legislative process. Unlike the law of the convention, the law in the technical annexes could be amended by a qualified majority of votes and from the time of its adoption (notification) was binding on all members. This method proved irreconcilable with universal membership in CINA, as members who were not capable or ready to submit to majority decisions had no choice but to remain outside the organization. It is for this reason that ICAO introduced the procedure of contracting (opting) out for members who are not ready to accept one or another technical standard or its amendment. But both processes (CINA and ICAO) have this in common that they are not passed by multilateral treaty but adopted unilaterally. There is no need for individual ratification or approval of these standards or of their amendments to make them operative. On the other hand, any dissenting member of ICAO has the right to contract out individually after the particular standard (amendment) becomes operative (effective). It has been suggested that this type of process be called "quasi-legislative." A comparison of ICAO with WHO, WMO, and IMCO (Facilitation Convention) has shown that all these organizations have adopted the above process as providing a proper regulatory response to technical change.

The differences between the quasi-legislative process, as in those four organizations, lie in the degree of limitation on contracting out which is imposed on the freedom of individual states. The most far-reaching limitation appears in the International Sanitary Regulations (Article 107), which authorize the World Health Assembly to reject reservations of (contracting out) states if it considers them incompatible with the objectives of the Regulations. On the other hand, according to the ICAO Convention, half of the member states may prevent the coming into force of a standard adopted by the ICAO Council (two-thirds majority). This is quite normal since the twenty-seven members of the Council carry out a quasi-legislative function for all the members whose number is now more than one hundred. If less than half of the members oppose acceptance of the standard, the latter will become operative. The only escape for an individual dissenting state, then, is the contracting out procedure.

While the process of adoption or amendment of civil aviation standards has deviated fundamentally from traditional treaty processes by abandoning the contracting in method, maritime safety standards as laid down in the Safety of Life at Sea Convention (1960) and the Load Line Convention (1966) have not abandoned traditional treaty methods. Unlike the ICAO Annexes, which are not an integral part of the Chicago Convention, the Maritime Regulations are a part of the Maritime Conventions. The contracting parties have adopted the *pacta sunt servanda* rule, and there is no possibility of contracting out unilaterally once a standard is operative. The regulatory response in the field of civil aviation obviously calls for a more rapid process than the response in the field of maritime transport. These observations apply, however, only to the Safety of Life at Sea and the Load Line Conventions. As has been stated above, the procedures contained in the 1965 Maritime Facilitation Convention are similar to those applied to the ICAO Annexes.

Apart from processes of adoption of the technical law, certain procedures applicable in its implementation have been chosen for discussion. Of particular interest to international lawyers is the procedure governing the activities of the International Frequency Registration Board. It has been emphasized that ITU rejected the idea of establishing any legal title in frequencies, or even a right of priority of use of a frequency. Instead, the IFRB has undertaken the task of running an administrative and quasi-judicial machinery in order to maintain order in the world frequency spectrum. This mechanism relies on the allocation of frequency bands to various services as laid down in the Frequency Allocation Plan, and it provides for a process of inquiry into the assignment of individual frequencies by states to radio stations in their territories. This inquiry is of a quasi-judicial nature since all member states of ITU have the right to object to the international recognition or protection of a notified frequency if it does not conform to ITU law (the Convention, the Radio Regulations, and the Frequency Allocation Plan), and if it is likely to cause harmful interference to operating frequencies which already enjoy international recognition and protection, *de jure* or *de facto*. *De jure* protection is the privilege of frequencies which, after having passed the examination of the board, are registered in column 2a, the column of protected frequencies. *De facto* protection is accorded to frequencies which did not pass the examination because of some defect and are registered in column 2b, but which do not, in practice, cause harmful interference to protected frequencies.

The Master Register, which is the responsibility of the Board, presents a reasonably complete picture of the frequency spectrum usage. Although the Board cannot compel a nonconforming state to withdraw or modify a harmful frequency, it can publicly ascertain the fact of harmfulness in the register and thus draw the attention of all member states to the violation of the public spectrum order. The state suffering injury from such violation may then challenge the lawbreaking state by resort to the ITU machinery for settling disputes, including compulsory arbitration, in accordance with the Optional Protocol of 1965.

With the exception of long-distance (HF) broadcasting, which is not within the protective machinery of ITU, any violation of the spectrum order in other essential fields of radiocommunication (safety services of maritime transport and civil aviation, fixed services of public correspondence, meteorology, and so on) would lead to complete chaos, which is hardly reconcilable with the requirements of the contemporary world.

In a discussion of procedures relating to the law of civil aviation, attention must be drawn to procedures in Annexes 11, 12, and 13 of the Chicago Convention. It has been shown that the organization of air traffic control on a world-wide scale (Annex 11) has a decisive impact on reducing national sovereignty in the airspace from a proprietary to a functional level. The same is true of the role of Annexes 12 and 13 (search, rescue, and accident inquiry). Particular attention has been drawn to the elaborate procedure of accident inquiry. The above procedures have been instrumental in securing better standards of safety and efficiency of air services. The objective of the endorsement procedures relating to airworthiness and personnel licenses (Articles 39 and 40 of the Chicago Convention) is the same, but in practice there was no resort to these procedures.

Finally, the procedure of issuing safety and load line certificates, as provided in the relevant maritime conventions, is of special interest. In contrast to the IFRB procedure, where the international function is centralized and carried out by an international organ, this procedure is decentralized and carried out by national authorities acting in both national and international capacity (*dédoublement fonctionnel*). The certificates of safety issued by these authorities under the provisions of the relevant conventions create a presumption of compliance of a ship and its equipment with the safety standards set out in the conventions. But ships in foreign harbors, that is, in harbors of other contracting parties, are subject to verification. If the presumption of compliance proves incorrect, the ships can be detained until the verifying authority is satisfied with the improvements in the safety conditions. In principle these are not direct institutional sanctions imposed on law-breaking member states by any of the organizations.[3] The UPU Convention, for example, authorizes member states to apply individual sanctions in the nature of enforcement measures against member states which disregard the right to freedom of transit of mail. Similarly, the two IMCO Conventions authorize a member state to detain the ships of other contracting states. Disputes between states can be settled by the use of the compulsory arbitration machinery (UPU, ITU, and ICAO). Otherwise, the observance of a communication regime may be of a self-mandatory character, particularly in the fields of telecommunication and postal services. In this case the self-imposed sanction is not strictly of a legal character, but it is nevertheless *de facto* effective and may lead to the establishment of new international usages.

The variety of procedures applied in the fields of global communication have called for various organs to carry out the necessary functions relating to the creation or application of the technical law. In the same way in which some of these procedures have deviated from traditional treaty law, the work of these organs has deviated from methods of classic diplomacy and tends to establish a new category of what has been called expert or technical diplomacy. It is thanks to the new approach of the technical experts to international negotiation that some of the defects of the diplomatic bargaining methods have been avoided. The new approach may be characterized as a *normative* or cooperative approach, because in the negotiations emphasis is put on the creation of common standards of cooperation and behavior rather than on coexistence and on delimiting the conflicting interests of the negotiating sovereigns.

Among the expert organs in the fields of global communication may be found *inter alia* the Consultative Committees (Councils) of UPU and ITU, the Air Navigation Commission, the Air Transport Committee, and the Maritime Safety Committee. All these bodies are composed of experts and not career diplomats. This method of composition also applies to the executive organs of the agencies, in some cases to the exclusion of career diplomats, who are not experts in the particular field of communication (ITU).

Moreover, even the nonnegotiating organs which enjoy international status, such as chief executive (administrative) officers and the secretariats (including the IFRB), participate in the process of technical diplomacy. The chief executive officer maintains permanent liaison with member governments and in that respect acts on behalf of the particular organization. In member countries such liaison is maintained by technical ministries. Foreign offices exercise supervisory functions for political purposes, to the extent to which they are relevant in technical organizations. Thus the growth of the agencies of global communication has had a significant effect on the reorganization of national governments. The task of representing a member country abroad has ceased to be a foreign office monopoly, and the foreign office now shares with technical ministries the function of conducting technical negotiations and concluding and implementing agreements of a technical nature. Foreign offices have retained the right of approving the appointment of the representatives of their countries to international organizations, who are proposed by the technical departments. They give them instructions of a political nature and they have a say in the conclusion of new international agreements, but they cannot obstruct the constructive drive toward uniformity of technical standards on which global communication depends for its development. In other fields different methods of international cooperation have appeared, such as international inspection (IAEA) or the methods adopted by ILO or IMF or by the Antarctic Treaty powers which shelved considerations of national sovereignty in order to achieve a measure of coordination.

Some of the agencies in the field of global communication have assumed legislative or quasi-legislative functions, and thus their organs concentrate on preparing legislative material and drafting texts. Since standards passed by these agencies do not require ratification or approval by member states, the responsibility of these organs goes further than that of ordinary administrative agencies.

The methods of technical diplomacy were transplanted from intergovernmental organizations to nongovernmental agencies which came to supplement the work of the former whenever intergovernmental bodies were unable to carry out a particular task. Thus IATA's rate-fixing machinery based on an interairline agreement operates on lines of private technical diplomacy, but IATA must be considered a mixed agency (public and private) since its rate-fixing decisions require the approval of the interested governments. Moreover, IATA has adopted the basic structure of a Specialized Agency of the United Nations. It is composed of a plenary organ, an executive organ, the secretariat under the chief executive officer, and the various expert organs. Among its administrative organs, the clearing house is of considerable importance. It settles interairline accounts in a way which is similar to the UPU clearing system. The latter settles accounts of postal administrations regarding the payment of transit charges.

Another mixed agency is INTELSAT, which operates in the field of commercial satellite telecommunication. Although it is based on an intergovernmental agreement (Washington, 1964), the member states are represented either by governments or by nongovernmental telecommunication administrations (corporations) as the case may be. The principal Washington agreement is accompanied by a supplementary agreement concluded by governments as well as by nongovernmental entities. The twin Washington agreements are of an interim character and are likely to be replaced by a permanent arrangement in the near future.[4] Attention has been drawn to some of the INTELSAT problems which call for consideration, namely, the double responsibility of COMSAT, which is at the same time an agency (nongovernmental) representing the United States in the international system, and manager of the latter; the distribution of quotas and votes on lines of weighted voting; and the global participation of all states in the system. This is not likely to be achieved in view of the creation of a separate operational satellite telecommunication system by the Soviet Union (Intersputnik).

While certain organs of the agencies of global communication perform administrative and legislative functions, other organs were charged with the exercise of judicial or quasi-judicial functions. Among the judicial organs, those applying the arbitration procedure are the most frequent. Compulsory arbitration was first introduced by UPU and later adopted by ITU, ICAO, and INTELSAT. But the practice of these organizations shows that resort to arbitration is extremely rare and that the methods of informal settlement of disputes by the chief executive officer (UPU) or by some other organ have proved preferable. Quasi-judicial functions are carried out by the ICAO Council and by the IFRB. IMCO asked the International Court of Justice for the settlement of one of its vital problems by advisory opinion (elections to the Maritime Safety Committee). All Specialized Agencies, except UPU, may directly ask the International Court of Justice for an advisory opinion, but with the exception of ILO and IMCO none of them have done so.

After a discussion of the legal status of the operational space of communication and its impact on the organization of services, of the procedures of generating and implementing the technical law of communication, and of the organs in charge of this function, attention has been drawn to the nationality of vehicles of communication and the legal regime on board the vehicle. The details of such a legal regime and the position of persons, cargo, and events governed by it are beyond the scope of this inquiry, which is concerned with public international law aspects. But vehicles of global communication carry their nationality abroad into the territory of other member states. Therefore international law is concerned with the method of assignment of nationality to a vehicle, that is, with the transaction which links the particular vehicle with a particular system of municipal law and the legal consequences of the link for the vehicle operating on international routes.

It has been recalled that the procedure of establishing such a link originated from the national registration of ships. Registration of ships, aircraft, or satellites does not create new national territory. Vehicles of communication remain movable property although persons, cargo, and events on board the vehicle may be governed by the law of registration. The law of the flag in force on board ships may justify the classification of ships as pseudoterritory (largely a misnomer), but it is hardly possible to transfer the idea to aircraft or satellite. Be that as it may, two concepts have prevailed as to the registration of vehicles of communication by states. According to the first, states have complete autonomy of granting their nationality to a vehicle, and according to the second, international regulation may impose restrictions on this autonomy. Thus Article 5 of the Geneva Convention on the High Seas restricts the discretion of states by requiring the existence of a genuine link between the ship and the registering state. But this "anti-flag of convenience" attitude of the contracting parties to the convention was not shared by the International Court of Justice in the advisory opinion relating to IMCO. The Court bypassed the issue of flags of convenience and accepted the registered tonnage of states (irrespective of any link) as a decisive factor for elections to the Maritime Safety Committee. This leaves international lawyers with an unsolved problem. For, while states have complete autonomy of registration of ships for purposes of certain provisions of the IMCO Convention, their autonomy may be restricted for other purposes as envisaged in Article 5 of the Geneva Convention on the High Seas, as well as beyond the purposes of Article 28 of the IMCO Convention.

The situation is similar in various municipal laws. Some states, the United States and the United Kingdom, insist on the fulfillment of certain requirements in the process of registration, such as the nationality of the owner or the genuine link in the meaning of Article 5 of the Geneva Convention on the High Seas. Other states such as Liberia and Panama have adopted the "convenience" approach. They defended this approach in the proceedings before the International Court of Justice in the IMCO case.

In the field of international civil aviation the situation is even more complicated. First of all, the various texts refer to the nationality of aircraft and on other occasions to the nationality of airlines. This creates a considerable confusion and calls for rectification. While the Two Freedom Agreement and the Five Freedom Agreement refer to the nationality of aircraft, the model bilateral transport agreement insists, for certain purposes, on the genuine nationality of airlines. Thus the substantial ownership and effective control requirement in the Bermuda (model) Agreement entitles states to revoke the operating permit of airlines of any other contracting state which disregards the above requirement. As to the nationality of aircraft, the Chicago Convention has adopted the principle of complete autonomy of states in the registration process. It has been suggested that the emancipation of aircraft, as well as of ships, from restrictions on national registration (nationality of free choice) may contribute to a better distribution of resources of global communication all over the world, particularly to the advantage of the developing countries.

As to conflicts between the law of registration of the vehicle of communication and the territorial law of the state in which the vehicle finds itself on its international route, the general rule is that the law of registration in force inside the vehicle prevails over the territorial law as long as events inside the vehicle produce no effects outside the vehi-

cle. This is particularly so whenever such events do not offend the public order of the receiving state. In this connection the danger of lawlessness on board civil aircraft has been considered. Decisions of municipal
courts of the United Kingdom and the United States have not
diminished the threat of such lawlessness, and the Tokyo Convention of
1964 constitutes a doubtful remedy. On the one hand the Tokyo Convention gives priority to the law of registration, but on the other, it permits the application of other systems of law, including the territorial
law, without assuring absolute conditions of punishment or extradition
of persons who have committed offenses on board aircraft. In this respect the situation is different from the legal regime on board ship,
which follows the law of the flag and presumably on board satellite,
which, apart from the short period of launching and of splashdown,
finds itself in outer space beyond the reach of state sovereignty and thus
follows the law of registration.

It may be asked why global communication should be treated separately from regional or inland communication. The answer is that world
communication is a social reality which, because of its indivisibility, is
of special significance involving the whole family of nations and the law
of nations as a universal legal system, irrespective of geography or political ideology. The routes of global communication were first opened
by the great explorers who circumnavigated the world in the sixteenth
century. Maritime intercourse is the earliest branch of global communication, although it has been the last to be institutionalized. UPU and
ITU institutionalized postal services and telecommunication in the early
half of the nineteenth century and CINA and ICAO followed after
World War I and World War II.

Various legal provisions were instrumental in promoting universality of membership. First, there was the concept of the "open union"
(union ouverte), which allowed all sovereign states to adhere unilaterally to the organization. Moreover, both UPU and ITU admitted non-
sovereign entities, such as overseas territories of European powers or of
the United States. Although the concept of the union ouverte was abandoned when the organizations of global communication became
Specialized Agencies of the United Nations and when United Nations
politics affected the membership problem, some of the agencies extended their membership through admitting associate members, which

were often semisovereign countries. UPU allowed members who were unable to ratify a revised convention to adhere to the global postal regime by implied ratification. This has remained an extratreaty principle. Finally, even states or governments which are formally outside the agencies of global communication (nonsignatories) participate *de facto* in their network through bilateral agreements with member states and informal contacts with the headquarters of the agencies.

It can be inferred from the advisory opinion of the International Court of Justice in the Reparation of Injuries case that if the vast majority of the family of nations adheres to an organization the latter enjoys the benefits of objective international personality. Its personality in international law is valid not only vis-à-vis members but *erga omnes*— with global legal validity. This rule applies not only to the United Nations but also to the Specialized Agencies.

The regulatory response to the challenge of technical progress in the field of global communication has been successful largely because of its capacity of abandoning orthodox procedures, if no longer suitable, and creating new legal formulations which have contributed to the efficiency and safety of communication services. The need for a uniform technical law in the various branches of global communication often constitutes an uncomfortable pressure on states which are unable to adjust their municipal laws and institutions to international standards. While they are ready to take steps to this effect, time is often needed to bring about the necessary adjustments. Hence the dilemma connected with quasi-legislative procedures which, on the one hand, provide an immediate response to technical change but, on the other, may often cause delay in the universal acceptance of standards.

To enable all member states of the family of nations to join in a global regime of communication, international standards are not treated as legally binding but are generally recognized as paralegal measures. We have seen in the discussion of ICAO, WHO, WMO, and IMCO (Facilitation Convention) that standards (amendments), if passed by a qualified or simple majority of votes, become operative (effective) immediately for all members without need of ratification or approval. Consequently, the presumption arises that all states will comply with them. But such a presumption is not irrebuttable and if a state does not in fact comply with a standard, it will opt out by notification to the organization. While such notification is legally binding, the standard, in spite of its operativeness, is not. This is a jurisprudential anomaly, but it provides a reasonable way of reconciling the requirements of immediate regulatory response to technical progress with universality of participation.

While dissenting members in this way gain time for adjusting their technical and legal position to the necessary international standards, they are, despite their dissent, allowed to remain members of the particular organization. The situation is different in the field of postal services and telecommunication, as well as in the maritime safety conventions which follow, with certain exceptions, the traditional treaty procedures. Both legal solutions now exist side by side in the field of global communication.

But although they exist side by side, the paralegal system is symptomatic of the whole law of world communication. It may indicate a wider trend in the development of contemporary international law, that is, the growing and often inescapable dependence of states on participation in activities of global and indivisible concern, where the principal sanction is exclusion from participation of those states that refuse to comply with universally accepted standards.[5]

NOTES

INTRODUCTION

1. See note 22, VII.

2. Friedmann, *The Changing Structure of International Law* (1964).

CHAPTER ONE
THE LEGAL STATUS OF THE OPERATIONAL COMMUNICATION SPACE AND ITS IMPACT ON THE ORGANIZATION OF GLOBAL SERVICES

1. Alexandrowicz, *An Introduction to the History of the Law of Nations in the East Indies, 16th, 17th and 18th Centuries* (1967).

2. McDougal and Burke, *The Public Order of the Oceans* (1962), pp. 104–15.

3. The convention applies on the basis of reciprocity but it does not include fishing vessels, warships, and vessels exercising any kind of public authority. Article 16 provides for certain exceptions to equal treatment. See McDougal and Burke, *id.*, p. 112.

4. See Anglo-Norwegian Fisheries Case, [1951], *I.C.J. Reports,* 116.

5. See Colombos, *International Law of the Sea* (1967); Marx, "Regulation of International Liner Shipping and Freedom of the Seas," *Journal of Industrial Economics* (November, 1967).

6. Colombos, *supra* note 5, pp. 393–95.

7. Padwe, "The Curriculum of IMCO," *International Organisation,* Vol. XIV (1960).

8. See opposition of India, Greece, and the Scandinavian countries to IMCO jurisdiction in economic affairs, Padwe, *id.*

9. IMCO has to its credit a number of conventions, and it discharges certain functions in the implementation of the following instruments: the Convention for the Safety of Life at Sea (1948); the International Regulations for preventing Collisions at Sea (1948); the Convention for the Safety of Life at Sea (1960); the Convention for the Prevention of the Pollution of the Sea by Oil (1954); Conferences relating to the above convention in 1962; Maritime Facilitation Convention (1965) and the Load Line Convention (1966). See Annual Reports of IMCO, 1965–1966. In 1969 the International Convention on the Tonnage Measurement of Ships was concluded and in the same year the International Legal Conference on Maritime Pollution adopted two conventions, one relating to Intervention on the High Seas in cases of Oil Pollution Casualties and the other on Civil Liability for Oil Pollution Damage.

10. Other factors are continental shelf activities and the extension of maritime zones. See also the right of a coastal state to take measures on the high seas to prevent, mitigate, or eliminate grave and imminent danger to its coastline from pollution or threat of pollution of the sea by oil. The convention states that the above measures cannot affect the freedom of the high seas (Annual IMCO Report, 1969).

11. The United States adhered to the American Convention on Commercial Aviation of February, 1928.

12. Emphasis added.

13. Paragraph 2 of Article II adopted the principle of nondiscrimination between the contracting parties. It stated: "Regulations made by a contracting State as to the admission over its territory of the aircraft of other contracting States shall be applied without distinction of nationality."

14. But see the limitation on the freedom of passage imposed by Article 3 (below).

15. Protocol of amendments to various articles: 3, 5, 7, 15, 34, 37, 41, 42, etc. opened for signature on June 15, 1929. Hudson, *International Legislation,* Vol. I, p. 384.

16. The Chicago Convention was signed on December 7, 1944, and it came into force on April 4, 1947. PICAO was the provisional agency.

17. The text does not say "every contracting State" but refers to "every State," which transcends the bounds of the convention. We may presume that it is declaratory of a rule of international customary law.

18. It has been argued that although the airspace over the high seas is not under the sovereignty of states, the latter can nevertheless establish a "contiguous airspace" to which they would extend their control over foreign aircraft coming from the high seas toward their national airspace. This extension of jurisdiction (not of sovereignty) unilaterally imposed is exercised in the interest of national security. See Cheng, *The Law of International Air Transport* (1962), and Hayton, "Jurisdiction of the Littoral State in the Air Frontier," 3 *Philippine Int'l. L.J.,* p. 369 (1964).

19. It states: "Each contracting State agrees that all aircraft of the other contracting States, being aircraft not engaged in scheduled international air services shall have the right, subject to the observance of the terms of this Convention, to make flights into or in transit non-stop across its territory and to make stops for non-traffic purposes without the necessity of obtaining prior permission, and subject to the right of the State flown over to require landing. . . ." Article 5 further states: "Such aircraft, if engaged in the carriage of passengers, cargo, or mail for remuneration or hire other than scheduled international air services, shall also, subject to the provisions of Article 7 [relating to cabotage], have the privilege of taking on or disembarking passengers, cargo, or mail, subject to the right of any State where such embarkation or discharge takes place to impose such regulations, conditions or limitations as it may consider desirable."

20. A multilateral European agreement on commercial rights of nonscheduled air services has been concluded on a regional basis in 1956. See McNair, *The Law of the Air* (1964), p. 13. Among the rights granted under the 1956 agreement are transit rights and traffic rights of a nonrevenue character, revenue traffic rights, emergency and humanitarian flights, taxi flights with a low-seating capacity, and charter flights. See Cheng, *supra* note 18, p. 214.

21. As to the sixth and seventh freedom of the air, see Cheng, *supra* note 18, p. 13 f. The sixth freedom extends to carriage of traffic between two foreign countries via the home state of the carrier (not including cabotage). The seventh freedom covers traffic carried by an airline operating entirely outside the home state. Cabotage is defined in Article 7 of the ICAO Convention, which states that "each contracting State shall have the right to refuse permission to the aircraft of other contracting States to take on in its territory passengers, mail and cargo carried for remuneration or hire and destined for another point within its territory. Each contracting State undertakes not to enter into any arrangements which specifically grant any such privilege on an exclusive basis to any other State or an airline of any other State, and not to obtain any exclusive privilege from any other State."

22. Cheng, *supra* note 18, p. 25.

23. Circular 63–AT/6.

24. Pyman, "Australia and International Air Law," in *International Law in Australia* (D. O'Connell ed. 1965). Another clause in the bilateral agreements is the "grant of right" clause in which the contracting parties grant each other the right to operate international air services on agreed routes. In the United States the permit was granted to foreign air carriers (as well as domestic enterprises) by the CAB. The latter was composed of five members appointed by the President of the United States for six-year terms with the advice and consent of the Senate. Permits are issued with the approval of the President. The CAB can prescribe terms, conditions, limitations, and the duration of the permit (see Federal Aviation Act, 49 U.S.C. § 1372(e)(1958)). It can modify, amend, suspend, or cancel the permit if the public interest so requires (§ 1372(f)). Under § 1502, the CAB must act consistently with obligations assumed by the United States under bilateral agreements with foreign states. All functions, powers, and duties of the CAB and the chairman, members, officers, and offices thereof were transferred in 1966 to the Secretary of Transportation by

Pub.-L. 89–670, 80 Stat. 931, 49 U.S.C. 1654, 1655(d), 1657(f),(g), to be exercised by the National Transportation Safety Board (NTSB). Bilateral agreements are treated as executive agreements rather than as treaties and do not require the advice and consent of the Senate. See Lissitzyn, "Bilateral Agreements on Air Transport," 30 *J. Air L. & Com.,* p. 248 (1964); Lissitzyn, "International Aspects of Air Transport in American Law," 33 *J. Air L. & Com.,* p. 86 (1967); Calkins, "Acquisition of Operating Authority by Foreign Air Carriers," 31 *J. Air L. & Com.,* p. 65 (1965). As to the conflict between the United States and the United Kingdom over the Tokyo route, see Cheng, *supra* note 18, p. 368. As to the controversy between BOAC (SAS, KLM, SABENA) and CAB, see Kittrie, "United States Regulation of Foreign Airlines Competition," 29 *J. Air L. & Com.,* p. 1 (1963). Capacity is determined by the size of the aircraft (particularly calculated by the number of passenger seats) multiplied by the frequency of services in a particular period of time. Some countries (e.g., the United Kingdom) tend to pursue a liberal policy in respect of capacity requirements but a strict policy in respect of the grant of routes. Cheng. *supra* note 18, p. 403.

25. Cheng, *supra* note 18, p. 424. Certain countries for a long time used the predetermination formula, for example, Australia in her bilateral air transport agreements with Canada (1946), Pakistan (1949), India (1949), the Netherlands (1951), Lebanon (1953), and South Africa (1955). Pyman, *supra* note 24. Similarly the United Kingdom had concluded bilateral agreements on a fifty-fifty division of traffic with Argentina, Eire, France (metropolitan), and Turkey.

26. Wassenbergh, *Post-war International Civil Aviation and the Law of the Air* (1962), p. 60.

27. Cheng, *supra* note 18, p. 429.

28. Cheng, *supra* note 18, p. 554.

29. Predetermination shares in the overall traffic are not a flexible solution.

30. In case of "through services" permission is granted to a foreign airline to operate beyond the territory of the grantor state into the territory of third states (beyond points). Cheng, *supra* note 18, p. 399.

31. Lissitzyn, "Bilateral Agreements on Air Transport," 30 *J. Air L. & Com.,* p. 248 (1964).

32. But *ex post facto* review is applied only in case of abuse of discretion. Cheng, *supra* note 18, pp. 429, 434. A stopover made by a passenger en route does not affect the "freedom identity" of the traffic (third, fourth, and fifth freedom), which is determined by the points of departure and destination marked in the ticket. Wassenbergh, *supra* note 26, p. 121.

33. Wassenbergh, *supra* note 26, p. 67.

34. Although it is insignificant in practice. See footnote below.

35. But there are numerous companies running nonscheduled and semischeduled air services.

36. Annex 11:2,3.

37. Annex 11:2,5,2,1.

38. Annex 11:2,5,2,2,1. As to new developments, see Supplement, 5th ed., February 1, 1967.

39. The crew of an aircraft in flight communicates with ground stations to give details concerning its position and to receive instructions relating to the position of other aircraft and the conditions of the flight areas. The radio connection between aircraft and traffic control is continuous.

40. See Annex 11:3,4,2,1, and 3,5.

41. Annex 11:3,6,2. A flight plan must be submitted on behalf of an aircraft to the Air Traffic Control Unit (Chapter 3 of Annex 2). According to the system of positive ground control, flight plans are approved by a government controller before take-off. Alterations in a flight plan must also be sanctioned by the controller. A number of countries adopted the above system. Under United States ground control, alterations of the flight plan (if the plane is flying under visual flight rules) can be submitted to the ground staff of the appropriate airline which will notify the government controller. ICAO allows both systems.

42. Annex 11:3,6,3.

43. In 1957 a Flight Information Region was established in Tegucigalpa (Honduras). It covers the Central American Region and supplies air traffic radio aids and radio communication services to civil aviation in the region. In 1960 the "Compagnie des Services de Navigation Aérienne de l'Amerique Centrale" was created with the object of exclusive exploitation of navigational services, telecommunication services, and aids to navigation in the Central American Region. Similar institutions were established in Africa, that is, l'ASECNA, covering the French-speaking African Republics, and EUROCONTROL, established in 1960. The latter is the European Organization for the safety of air navigation. It is operated as a public service with the participation of the United Kingdom, France, Germany, Ireland, and the Benelux States. It established a common control agency. See Guinchard, "La coopération entre Etats pour le contrôle de la circulation aérienne, 7 *Ann. Fran. Droit Int'l*, p. 450 (1961).

44. Chapter 5 distinguishes three phases: the uncertainty phase, the alert phase, and the distress phase.

45. Chapter 6 requires, whenever possible, the use of radio telephony for air-ground communication.

46. See Legal Committee, 14th Session, Documents, Vol. II (1963), pp. 158–89.

47. The task assigned to air traffic services has, in most countries, been considered a public service and the trend is to have them operated by government agencies.

48. *ICAO Bulletin*, Vol. XX, No. 6 (1965).

49. Campbell, "Possible Uses of Satellites for Navigation and Traffic Coordination," *ICAO Bulletin*, No. 3 (1964).

50. See Annex 11:3,11; 3,1,2.

51. As to succession of new states to the rights and duties of the colonial powers in respect of civil aviation, see Mankiewicz, "Air Law Conventions and the New States," 29 *J. Air L. & Com.,* p. 52 (1963).

52. Annex 11:2,7.

53. Annex 11:2,1,1.

54. The operational requirements of civil aviation compel control authorities all over the world to act across national frontiers which lead to the establishment of new usages in international air law.

55. As to the distinction between scheduled and nonscheduled services in practice, see Articles 9 and 15 of the ICAO Convention.

56. See "Manual of the ICAO Standard Atmosphere," 2nd ed., 1969. The standard atmosphere, extending to about 32 Km above earth, has been adopted by ICAO for technical purposes, but indirectly it relates also to the legal significance of the boundary between atmosphere and exoatmosphere. See also the work carried out by experts of Aeropanel, established by ICAO.

57. Report published in 1967, p. 166 f. An excellent discussion of the relevant problems can be found in Fawcett, *International Law and the Use of Outer Space* (1968) and in Jenks, *Space Law* (1965). See also McDougal, Lasswell, and Vlasic, *Law and Public Order in Space* (1963).

58. There have also been bilateral agreements relating to nonscheduled flights, for example, the Franco-Spanish Agreement of 1948, the Franco-Italian Agreement of 1950, the British-Swiss Agreement of 1952, and further agreements. If a state is neither a contracting party to such a bilateral agreement nor to a regional multilateral agreement relating to nonscheduled services, it can still operate its aircraft on noncommercial (nonscheduled) flights into the airspace or territory of another contracting party to the ICAO Convention without prior permission (Article 5,1). However, prior permission is required in case of commercial nonscheduled flights (Article 5,2). There is a tendency for states to insist in most cases on prior permission, even in relation to noncommercial flights, for fear of being faced with the presence of foreign aircraft on a scheduled service in disguise. The United Kingdom government stated that if a precise definition of scheduled services could be agreed, prior permission could be abandoned. See Jennings, "International Civil Aviation and the Law," 22 *Brit. Y. B. Int'l L.,* p. 191 (1945). Such a definition was later adopted by the ICAO Council but it has not removed the fear of cryptoscheduled flights in practice.

59. With the rapid progress of aircraft, outdated aircraft are used by nonscheduled services the volume of which is growing. Thus the problem of cryptoscheduled flights is gaining significance.

60. In the past the term *ether* has been used. See Joeden, "Die Funksendefreiheit der Staaten," 3 *Jahrbuch für Internationales Recht* p. 85 (1954); 4 *id.,* (1954) 71.

61. Sibert, *Traité de droit international public,* Vol. I (1951), p. 848.

62. Author's translation.

63. Oppenheim, *International Law* (8th ed. Lauterpacht 1955), Vol. I, p. 529.

64. *Id.*

65. Joeden, *supra* note 60.

66. Codding, *The International Telecommunication Union* (1952), p. 187.

67. Some light is thrown on this question in the Geneva Plan for an International Broadcasting Union (IBU, 1926). In the European Allocation Plan the following rules were considered important in the process of allocation of frequencies: (1) Older stations should be affected by the plan as little as possible; (2) Stations of major national and international importance should enjoy at least one exclusive allocation in the more desirable frequencies; (3) Separation by distance is important. This plan shows more clearly why the "priority" rule could not be an overriding one. See Codding, *supra* note 66, p. 92.

68. Codding, *supra* note 66, p. 190.

69. Goy, "La répartition des fréquences en matière de télécommunication," 5 *Ann. Fran. Droit Int'l*, p. 569 (1959).

70. The engineered spectrum of 1947 was later replaced by an evolutionary approach. Leive, "Regulating the Use of the Radio Spectrum," *Telecommunication Journal* (June, 1970).

71. But see the views of the vice-president of COMSAT, John A. Johnson, on the legal status of synchronous telecommunication satellites and their legal protection. "International Co-operation in Satellite Communications Systems" [1967] *Proc. Am. Soc. Int'l L.*, p. 24.

72. Satellites are either passive or active. The first simply reflect messages back to earth (United States Echo series); the second receive messages from the ground and amplify and transmit them back.

73. Submarine cables were first laid in 1851 (Dover-Calais) and in 1866 from Ireland to Newfoundland. See Reinsch, *Public International Unions* (1911), p. 63; Woolf, *International Government* (1916). States can lay submarine cables from their territory to that of other states, and they can do so thanks to the regime of the freedom of the sea. In 1884 the Convention for the Protection of Submarine Cables was concluded. See 24 Stat. 989 (1884); *Treaties, Conventions, International Acts, Protocols and Agreements etc. between the United States and Other Powers: 1776–1909*, Vol. 2 (Malloy ed. 1910), p. 1949. Article 1 of the convention states that "it shall be applicable, outside the territorial waters, to all legally established submarine cables landed in the territories, colonies or possessions of one or more of the High Contracting Parties." According to Article II, breaking and injury of a submarine cable is a punishable offense and states undertook to introduce legislation to punish those guilty of infringement of Articles II, V, and VI (Article V and VI relate to vessels engaged in laying cables). Thus uniformity of municipal laws was aimed at. See Clark, *International Communication* (1931). The concept of protection of submarine cables lends itself to application for the protection of satellites.

74. UNESCO, *Space Communication and Mass Media* (Reports and Papers on Mass Communication, No. 41, 1963); and *Les Télécommunications par Satel-*

lites, Aspects juridiques, ed. by Centre National de la Recherche Scientifique (CNRS).

75. See Fawcett, *supra* note 57.

76. Reinsch, *supra* note 73; Woolf, *supra* note 73; Codding, *The Universal Postal Union* (1964); Menon, "The Universal Postal Union" in *International Conciliation,* No. 552 (March, 1965); Sasse, *Der Weltpostverein* (1959); Weber, "The UPU Today and Tomorrow," in *Union Postale,* No. 8 (August, 1963); Chaubert, *L'Union postale universelle* (1970).

77. As amended by the Tokyo Convention, 1969. But the last available *Code Annoté* is that of the Vienna Acts of 1964.

78. As to Security Council sanctions relating to interruption of postal and other communication services, see Article 41 of the UN Charter. The provisions of the charter prevail over the provisions of the UPU and other treaty texts.

79. See Article 6 of the convention and Article 104 of the Executive Regulations to the convention. But according to Article III of the final protocol of the convention each member country has the option of increasing by 60 per cent or reducing by 20 per cent at most the charges prescribed in Article 16 (1) of the convention.

80. But as to restricted Postal Unions, the principle of nondiscrimination does not exclude the special privileges which member states concede to each other through the establishment of such Unions (Article 8 of the UPU Constitution). The member states of the restricted Unions tend to reduce the international postal charges to the level of domestic rates. Among the restricted Unions are the Postal Union of the Americas and Spain, the Postal Union of the Northern (Scandinavian) countries, the Arab Postal Union, and so on. Some of these Unions have extended their activities from postal services to telecommunication, for example, the African Union (Brazzaville) and the Balkan Union.

81. Members of the general public enter into contract for the carriage of mail with a postal agency. The provisions of such a contract are determined by *jus cogens* as laid down in the convention.

82. The above agreements are the Special Agreements, which deal separately with branches of postal services other than the letter post: Agreements concerning Postal Money Orders and Postal Travelers' Checks (established 1878); Insured Letters and Boxes (1878); Parcel Post (1880); Collection of Bills (1885); Postal Identity Cards; Subscription to Newspapers and Periodicals; Savings Bank Services. When the letter post is employed, it covers letters, single and reply-paid postcards, printed papers, literature for the blind, samples of merchandise, small packets, and phonopost items. See Article 15 of the convention.

83. About fifty years ago Persia (a member of UPU) complained that the United States and the United Kingdom were sending thousands of bibles to Persia while the latter did not send the Koran to Europe and America. The UPU made provision for Persia's complaint in Article V of the Convention of 1906. Woolf, *supra* note 73, p. 123.

84. At the Madrid Congress in 1920 and the Cairo Congress in 1924; later at the London Congress in 1929 and the Cairo Congress in 1934.

85. The Tokyo Convention of 1969 added a new article (Article 49) to the text which introduced an important change. It states that any administration which receives from another administration a greater quantity of mail than it actually sends to the latter has the right to claim compensation from the sending administration for covering its costs connected with the transport of mail (received), its sorting out, and delivery. This compensation is fifty centimes for 1 Kg of mail. If the annual accounts between the two administrations do not exceed 2000 francs, the sending administration has no obligation to pay compensation. An administration is free not to claim such compensation.

86. Article 1 of the convention refers to free transit of air mail. The proposal made at the Ottawa Congress aimed at the exemption of airmail transport from restrictions imposed on the fifth freedom of the air. See IMCO Document A-10-WP/23, EC/3, August 15, 1956, Res. A 10–32.

87. Res. C 30 II, 535, *Code Annoté*, p. 86.

88. Earlier a UPU arbitration court had condemned the action of a country of destination of mail in which a letter was opened for fiscal reasons because of suspicion of insertion of negotiable instruments in it (*Code Annoté*).

89. Reinsch, *supra* note 73, pp. 175–83.

90. *Id.* at p. 177.

91. *Id.* at p. 182.

92. These provisions do not apply in the case of a blockade.

93. The UPU Convention contains a code governing legal relations resulting from the operation of postal services, whether of a public or private character. See, for example, Article 4 (relating to the ownership of postal items which belong to the sender until delivery), Article 39 (responsibility in case of loss of registered mail—Article 40 of the Tokyo Convention), or Article 41 (responsibility of the sender—Article 42 of the Tokyo Convention). The ITU Convention rejects the notion of responsibility of the organs of international telecommunication services toward users. See also Article 13 of the Special Agreement relating to INTELSAT, 1964.

CHAPTER TWO

THE TECHNICAL LAW AND THE LAWMAKING PROCESSES

1. See Article 34(c).

2. Amendments had to be adopted by a three-fourths majority of the member states and by two-thirds of the total possible vote which could be cast if all members were represented.

3. Article 34(g).

4. Article 34 requires a majority of "at least two-thirds of the total possible vote."

5. Article 34.

6. Represented on the Commission.

7. See Shotwell, *The Origin of the International Labour Organisation*, Vol. I (1934), p. 148.

8. Air services in the United States started in 1918 when the Post Office Department inaugurated an airmail service between Washington D. C. and New York City. In 1925 the Post Office turned over the enterprise to private corporations. In 1926 Congress passed the Air Commerce Act. In 1934 the Aeronautics Branch of the Commerce Department was replaced by the Bureau of Air Commerce. In 1938 an independent Civil Aeronautics Authority was established, and in 1940 CAB (Civil Aeronautics Board) was created. The Board is an independent regulatory agency. See Cary, "Civil Aviation in the United States," *ICAO Bulletin*, Vol. XXI, No. 10 (1966); see also Nos. 3 to 5 (1966). The CAB was succeeded by the NTSB in 1966. See Ch. I, note 24, *supra*.

9. Lissitzyn, *International Air Transport and National Policy* (1942), p. 414. Professor Lissitzyn states, in relation to the Paris Convention of 1919: "Among the objections to the Convention expressed by Americans was the assertion that the delegation to a majority of the International Commission of the power to amend the technical annexes would constitute a delegation of legislative powers contrary to the United States Constitution." *Id.*, p. 414. The United States adhered to the Panamanian Convention on Commercial Aviation concluded at Havana in 1928. But no permanent international organization dealing with civil aviation was established by the convention. *Id.* at p. 370–71.

10. Merle, "Le pouvoir réglementaire des institutions internationales," 4 *Ann. Fran. Droit Int'l*, p. 341 (1958).

11. Bowett, *The Law of International Institutions* (1963), p. 330. The author draws our attention to the application of the "consent" principle or alternatively the "legislative" principle in amendment procedures, the first being employed in Article 94(a) of the ICAO Convention, the second in the UN Charter (Article 108), and in the Convention of WHO (Article 7), UNESCO (Article 13), and IAEA (Article 18). In other cases a combination of both principles had been adopted, for example, in UPU (Article 29 of the convention), but this has been changed at Vienna (Article 30 of the Constitution).

12. Alexandrowicz, *World Economic Agencies—Law and Practice* (1962), p. 133.

13. The terminology used in Chapter VI is not consistent. The title of Article 37 refers to international standards and procedures and the text of Article 37 to regulations, standards, and procedures. However, the title of the chapter refers to international standards and recommended practices.

14. Amendments are adopted by a majority of votes.

15. They could also depart from them before they become effective.

16. Merle, *supra* note 10.

17. See Oppenheim, *International Law*, Vol. I (8th ed. Lauterpacht 1955), paragraph 512.

18. A majority of states must notify their disapproval before the date of applicability of Annexes (amendments). Otherwise the latter become applicable. Individual notifications of departure from Annexes must be submitted after the date of applicability (*ICAO Bulletin*, Vol. XXI, No. 3 (1965).

19. Seyersted, "Settlement of Internal Disputes of Intergovernmental Organisations by Internal and External Courts," *Zeitschrift für Ausländisches Öffentliches Recht und Völkerrecht*, Vol. 24, No. 1 (February, 1964).

20. Organic law is established in the Constitution of the organization and can later be expanded by its organs.

21. Cheng, *The Law of International Air Transport* (1962), p. 65. But see Article 12 of the ICAO Convention according to which member states must accept the rules of the air established under the ICAO Convention as valid over the high seas.

22. See Cheng, *id.*, p. 66, who states that "a literal interpretation of this Article (38) would preclude member States from not following any amendment to an international standard if they have not given notice of their intention of doing so."

23. Uniformity is obviously necessary but allowance must be made for states which for one reason or another cannot comply with a standard, for lack of equipment or because an immediate adjustment of their system of civil aviation to international principles is not possible. If such states did not have the right of contracting out of inconvenient or unacceptable standards, they would have to abandon their membership in the organization. Technical assistance is often given to such states to enable them to catch up with technical development. Czechoslovakia, a member of ICAO, complained to the Tenth Session of the Assembly that she found it impossible to comply with the Annexes because she could not obtain the necessary equipment. She stated that the countries manufacturing the equipment were prohibited from exporting it to Czechoslovakia. The Technical Committee of ICAO considered the equipment essential for the safety and regularity of air traffic. The Assembly transferred the matter to the Council, which postponed the case. Mankiewicz, "L'Organisation Internationale de l'Aviation Civile," 3 *Ann. Fran. Droit Int'l*, pp. 383–417 (1957).

24. According to ICAO practice notification is also required for recommended practices whenever departure affects the safety or regularity of international air services. Sheffy, "The Air Navigation Commission of ICAO," 25 *J. Air L. & Com.*, p. 428, Vol. 25, Part II.

25. See Sheffy, *id.*

26. Schenkman, *International Civil Aviation Organisation* (1955), pp. 98, 257, 262. Professor Cheng expressed the view that standards are, in the absence of notification, binding. Cheng, *supra* note 21, at 70. But in his paper on "Centrifugal Tendencies in Air Law" (*Current Legal Problems*, Vol. 10 (1957) he states that a state is only indirectly under a duty to comply with a standard which it has notified it will no longer observe.

27. See Alexandrowicz, "The Convention on Facilitation of International Maritime Traffic and International Technical Regulation: A Comparative Study," 15

Int'l & Comp. L. Q., p. 625 (1966). In contrast with Regulations, conventions adopted by the Assembly require ratification or acceptance by member states (Article 20). According to Article 80 decisions made by the Assembly are passed by a majority of members present and voting. The adoption of conventions and agreements belong *inter alia* to this category.

28. The Soviet Union opposed this procedure as offending sovereignty. See Vignes, "Le réglement sanitaire international, aspects juridiques," 11 *Ann. Fran. Droit Int'l,* p. 699 (1965).

29. For the international control of spread of diseases, see "The New World Health Organization," 41 *Am. J. Int'l L.,* pp. 509, 526 (1947).

30. They have been amended in 1955, 1956, 1960, 1961, and 1965.

31. If a reservation is not withdrawn by the reserving state, the Regulations will not enter into force with respect to that state. In such a case the existing conventions and agreements listed in Article 105, to which the state is a party and which had been abrogated and replaced by the Regulations remain in force as far as the above state is concerned (compare Article 107 with Article IX,e of the Convention on the Safety of Life at Sea (1960), and with Article IX of the Maritime Facilitation Convention (1965)).

32. WMO Document, No. 183 T.P. 92 (1966).

33. *Weather Modification and the Law,* ed. by Taubenfeld (1968), p. 223.

34. As to Ocean stations, see above.

35. WMO Bulletin (April, 1967); *International Organisation* (Autumn, 1966), p. 842; *Year Book of the United Nations* (1964), p. 561.

36. See Articles 10 and 11 of the WMO Convention.

37. See also Fourth Meteorological Congress, WMO, No. 142 R.C.23, p. 94.

38. WMO Congress decided that recommended practices shall have the status of recommendations to members.

39. See also Regulations 101 and 102 (General Regulations).

40. But see exception in Article 12 of the ICAO Convention.

41. See Alexandrowicz, "The Convention on Facilitation of International Maritime Traffic and International Technical Regulation," 15 *Int'l & Comp. L. Q.,* p. 632 (1966).

42. Article VII lays down the methods of amendment, by simple or qualified majority of votes. Amendments come into force without ratification by states.

43. But see Resolution No. 2 of the Conference of 1965 as to the acceptance of standards. As to amendments, see Article VII(3).

44. In the case of Recommended Practices "should" is employed.

45. Alexandrowicz, *supra* note 41, p. 641.

46. The previous convention on the same subject was concluded in 1947.

47. Zacklin, *The Amendment of the Constitutive Instruments of the UN and the Specialised Agencies* (1968), pp. 30–47.

48. See Article 19 of the Convention of 1878.

49. For the reason of this anomaly, see below.

50. See Article 20 of the Convention of 1878.

51. See also *Code Annoté* referring to Article 25 of the Ottawa Convention.

52. Zacklin, *supra* note 47, pp. 32–39. As to amendments in the interval period (UPU), the author states that "a State which signified its disapproval . . . could not be bound by the amendments," *id*. at p. 47.

53. See Article 30 of the UPU Constitution, Article 94 of the ICAO Convention, and Article 52 of the IMCO Convention. The ITU Convention makes reference to revision in Article 6(2,h).

CHAPTER THREE

ADMINISTRATIVE AND QUASI-JUDICIAL PROCEDURES

1. Allocation of frequencies in the high frequency broadcasting bands proved impossible.

2. Long-range navigational aids had been developed during the war by the United States outside the Cairo allocations. In the new distribution of frequencies maritime safety services received the same number of frequencies as had been allocated to them in Cairo. Codding, *The International Telecommunication Union* (1952), p. 236.

3. As to defense services, members retain their entire freedom with regard to military radio installations. The word "retain" would indicate that members lost their freedom with regard to nonmilitary installations (Article 51, Montreux Convention).

4. Thus the spectrum is occupied in several ways: in frequency, in time, and in geographical location. See Glazer, "The Law-Making Treaties of the International Telecommunication Union Through Time and Space," 60 *Mich. L. Rev.*, p. 269 (1962).

5. The Extraordinary Administrative Radio Conference (Geneva, 1951) adopted for certain frequency bands (between 10 and 4000 Kc/s and frequency bands allocated exclusively to the maritime and aeronautical mobile services between 4000 and 28,000 Kc/s) a new International Frequency List (Plan). The original assignments based on this plan and forming the initial nucleus of the Master Register were supplemented by the assignments notified subsequently by member states of ITU and recorded by the IFRB.

6. See Article 9 of the Radio Regulations of 1959 (607).

7. As to various categories of services and allocations, see Article 5, Section II of the Radio Regulations, which distinguishes primary, permitted, and secondary services. Examples of the three services are fixed, radiolocation, and mobile services. While a fixed service is a service between fixed and specified points, a mobile service operates between mobile and land stations or between mobile stations (maritime, aeronautical). Section II contains rules relating to harmful interference in this hierarchy of stations.

8. Article 9 (486) of the Radio Regulations of 1959.

9. Article 9 (500–503) of the Radio Regulations and Article 48 of the ITU Convention.

10. See Article 9 of the Radio Regulations.

11. This procedure is also extended to cases under 503 (Art. 9, Radio Regulations). It is not intended to go into further details of the Regulations but it has to be kept in mind that each frequency assignment recorded in the Master Register bears a date in column 2c (the date of putting it into use) and a date in column 2a, 2b, or 2d (see exception in 576). The entries in 2a and 2b are in the frequency bands 573, 577, 582, 587, 589, 594, for which the Geneva Conference of 1951 adopted a new list. These initial assignments (as coordinated in the list) are supplemented by subsequent frequency notifications which are also covered by international protection. However, assignments for high frequency broadcasting and for the space services are entered in column 2d on the basis of notices, and they are not internationally protected. Cases of harmful interference, whenever they arise, are dealt with in accordance with the general provisions of 704 and 705 of the Regulations (Article 15), that is, members will exercise the utmost goodwill and mutual assistance to settle problems of harmful interference.

12. Reinforced by legal sanction in case of denial of transit (Article 2, Convention).

13. See Article 10 of the Radio Regulations. Although outer space frequencies are not within the normal spectrum protection of Article 9 of the Regulations (see Geneva Conference of 1963), ITU is likely to regularize the position in the near future (1971).

14. See dates in column c which are given for information only.

15. See Annual Report of IFRB (1969). The Master Register now contains the particulars of about 378,000 assignments.

16. See UN Charter (Article 2,7); the concept of matter essentially of international concern relates to cases of self-enforcement.

17. This conference was called Extraordinary Administrative Radio Conference (EARC) to allocate frequency bands for space radiocommunication purposes. It revised Article 9 of the Radio Regulations and added Article 9A, which especially refers to space and radio astronomy services. It set aside 15 per cent of the spectrum for satellite services and allocated frequency bands to space services of radio navigation, meteorology, research, and so on.

18. See Article 10 of the Radio Regulations; Codding, "Jamming and Protection of Frequency Assignments," 49 *Am. J. Int'l L.,* p. 384 (1955); Codding, *Broadcasting without Barriers* (1959).

19. That is, in bands enumerated in Nos. 573, 577, 582, 587, 589, and 594 in section III of Article 9.

20. Nos. 600, 603.

21. See statement made by M. Mili, secretary-general of ITU (*Telecommunication Journal ITU,* December 15, 1967); Annual Report ITU, 1968, and Report of Administrative Council of ITU, 1969, Document 3982-E, CA 25-2.

22. The following are the Annexes: (1) Personnel Licensing; (2) Rules of the Air; (3) Meteorology; (4) Aeronautical Charts; (5) Units of Measurement to be used in Air-Ground Communication; (6) Operation of Aircraft, International Commercial Air Transport; (7) Aircraft Nationality and Registration Marks; (8) Airworthiness of Aircraft; (9) Facilitation; (10) Aeronautical Telecommunication; (11) Air Traffic Control Services, Flight Information Services, Alerting Services; (12) Search and Rescue; (13) Aircraft Accident Inquiry; (14) Aerodromes; and (15) Aeronautical Information Services. Certain general rules on which the detailed codes in the Annexes are based are in the body of the Chicago Convention.

23. Annex 12:3, 1.

24. Annex 12:2, 11.

25. The main provisions of Annex 13 relate to the protection of evidence and the custody of the aircraft by the Inquiry State (3); the notification of the Registry State and the Manufacture State (4) which is defined as the state which first certified the particular aircraft type (see Accident Investigation Division, Report of Third Session, January 19–February 11, 1965, Document 8486, AIG, III) and inquiry, procedure, and report (5–6).

26. Annex 13:5,4.

27. Annex 13:5, 4, 1.

28. See Attachment B to Annex 13.

29. Among these groups can be distinguished: the Operation Group (responsible for the history of the flight and details about the flight crew); the Weather Group; the Air Traffic Control Group; the Witness Statement Group; the Flight Records Group; the Structure Group; the Powerplants Group; the Maintenance Record Group; the Human Factors Group, and the Examination, Search, and Fire Fighting Group.

30. The results of past inquiries have made an important contribution to the safety of international civil aviation. See ICAO Aircraft Accident Digest.

31. As to the functions of the Registry State in relation to certificates of airworthiness and personnel licenses, see Articles 31–33. The details of the endorsement procedure are contained in Articles 39–40.

32. It is submitted that the state of incorporation (registration) of the airline concerned has an equally important claim to admission to inquiries.

33. Without providing for the process of contracting out. Contracting out in the above sense should not be confused with the right of a state, participating in a multilateral agreement, to nonratification, nonapproval, or entering reservations (see UPU and ITU). As to the Safety of Life at Sea Convention, see Article IX relating to amendments of the convention and the Regulations. Amendments adopted in accordance with Article LX, b–c "shall come into force for all contracting governments except those which before it comes into force make a declaration that they do not accept the amendment." Thus nonacceptance should be declared before the amendment comes into force. The Assembly may, according to Article IX, e, determine that a nonaccepting state shall (upon expiry of the relevant period) cease to be a party to the convention (compare with WHO). The procedure of amendment is similar in the Load Line Convention (Article 29).

34. The standards dictated by the convention (Regulations) must be considered the minimum with which the Registry State must comply and the maximum which foreign states visited by vessels of the Registry State can require. The maximum-minimum formulation is the same as that adopted in the ICAO Annexes.

35. Adopted by the IMCO-sponsored Conference of 1966. In 1969 another IMCO-sponsored Conference adopted the International Convention on Tonnage Measurement which follows in general outline the principles of the Load Line Convention. The international tonnage certificate issued by a contracting state is accepted by the other contracting states. A procedure of control is provided and if a ship during its stay in a foreign harbor does not correspond with the data in the certificate, the flag state "shall be informed without delay" (Article 11). There is *no* right of detention of a ship. The Annexes to the convention containing the technical law are an integral part of the convention. Following the "Torrey Canyon" disaster the IMCO-sponsored Brussels Conference of 1969 adopted two conventions relating to oil pollution casualties and damage (IMCO Annual Report, 1969). See also footnote 10 (chapter I).

36. See Regulation 3 in Annex 1.

37. According to Article 4, the convention applies to ships registered in contracting states and to unregistered ships flying the flag of a state the government of which is a contracting government. According to Article 5 the convention does not apply to ships of war, to ships of less than a certain size, to pleasure yachts, and fishing vessels. According to Article 6, there is an exemption for ships on an international voyage between near neighboring ports of two or more states. According to Article 13, the survey, inspection, and marking of ships is carried out by officers of the appropriate administration. It can be entrusted to surveyors. According to Article 16, the international Load Line Certificate (1966) is issued to every ship which has been surveyed and marked. Some ships receive exemption certificates.

38. Alexandrowicz, "The Convention on Facilitation of International Maritime Traffic and International Technical Regulation," 15 *Int'l & Comp. L. Q.*, pp. 621, 627 (1966).

39. FAL/EG III/3, December 2, 1963, IMCO.

40. Alexandrowicz, *supra* note 38, p. 628.

41. FAL/EG II/7, May 6, 1963, IMCO.

42. FAL/EG I/SR 2, January 14, 1963, IMCO; FAL/EG II/2, April 3, 1963, IMCO.

43. Council XIV/35, May 6, 1965, E,IMCO (the convention came into force).

44. The Annex is divided into five sections: (1) Definitions of General Provisions; (2) Arrival, Stay, and Departure of Ship; (3) Arrival and Departure of Persons; (4) Public Health and Quarantine Including Sanitary Measures for Animals and Plants; (5) Miscellaneous Provisions. The Annex follows generally the outline of Annex 9 to the ICAO Convention. No other documentation except that mentioned in the Annex should be required from a ship and this covers the General Declaration, the Cargo Declaration, the Ship's Stores Declaration, the Crew's Ef-

fects Declaration, the Crew List, the Passenger List, the Documents required under the UPU Convention for Mail, and the Maritime Declaration of Health. The purpose and contents of these documents are defined in the Annex (section 2B) and a duty is imposed on the receiving harbor authorities to accept the documents as evidence of the facts stated in them. As to arrival and departure of persons, see Section 3 of the Annex.

45. Article II (1) introduces what may be called an international most favored transport clause. Thus the contracting states undertake that measures for facilitation of maritime transport shall be "not less favourable than measures applied in respect of other means of international transport," such as international air transport. A similar clause may be found in Annex 9 to the ICAO Convention (Chapter 2,2,1).

46. See Article VIII. The provisions relating to the amendment of the Convention are in Article IX. As to amendment of the Annex, see Resolution 4 of the London Conference of 1965 and Articles VII and VIII.

47. Annex 9:2,3.

48. See "General Negative Clause" in Standard 1(1) of the Annex, which states that "Public Authorities shall in all cases require only essential information to be furnished and shall keep the number of items to a minumum." But public authorities may call for further information in case of suspected fraud or in the interest of public order, public security, or public health, or to prevent the introduction or spread of diseases or pests affecting animals or plants.

49. See Annex 9, Chapter 2 (entry and departure of aircraft) distinguishing outbound and inbound procedures; Chapter 3 (entry and departure of persons); Chapter 4 (entry and departure of cargo and other articles). In each case the maximum of documents required is fixed. Chapters 4 through 8 deal with traffic, airports, and landing problems.

50. Section 4 and Chapter 8, respectively.

51. See also Standard 3(7) of the Annex, which deals with cases where evidence of protection against cholera, yellow fever, or smallpox is required from persons on board ship. The standard requires public authorities to accept the international certificate of vaccination or revaccination in the form provided for in the International Sanitary Regulations (see note 50, *supra*).

CHAPTER FOUR
TECHNICAL ORGANS AND EXPERT DIPLOMACY

1. But see the Convention on the Privileges and Immunities of the Specialised Agencies (Alexandrowicz, *World Economic Agencies*, p. 109).

2. As to voting procedures, see Articles 101 and 107 of the UPU General Regulations and Rules 14 and 15 of the ITU General Regulations.

3. As to the manner in which the plenary organ shares its prerogatives with Administrative Conferences, see Article 16 of the UPU Constitution and Article 7 of the ITU Convention.

4. As to arbitration, see Chapter V.

5. A clearing office was first established at the Vienna Conference in 1891, but clearing operations came to an end after World War I with the collapse of the gold standard. It was later reestablished, but only for transit charges and reply coupons (*Code Annoté*, p.125). The gold franc was adopted as a unit of account, and it has been maintained as such in Article 7 of the Vienna Constitution. Since the Brussels Convention of 1952, the clearing provisions have ceased to be called by that name though the liquidation of accounts, in essence, follows the same pattern.

6. *Code Annoté,* pp. 125,258,334. The administration concerned can also take advantage of the clearing system of the Bank of International Settlements in Basle. See Article 103 of the Executive Regulations. As to ITU, the establishment of a separate clearing house was proposed at the Madrid Conference in 1932, but the proposal was turned down. Article 101 of the Executive Regulations of UPU states that the settlement of postal accounts can be extended to telecommunication accounts. See Reinsch, *Public International Unions* (1911), p. 162; Codding, *International Telecommunication Union* (1952), p. 154, and Peaslee, *International Governmental Organizations* (1961). See also Article 40 of the Radio Regulations.

7. The executive organ had appeared earlier in the history of international organization as an isolated phenomenon only. For example, the Metrical Union had such an organ composed of fourteen members who were elected by the conference. See also the former International Institute of Agriculture in Rome and the Pan American Union, Reinsch, *supra* note 6, p. 15.

8. However, according to Article 17(2) of the UPU Constitution, even "members of the Executive Council carry out their functions in the name and in the interest of the Union." Article 9(1) of the Montreux Convention states: "In the interval between Plenipotentiary Conferences, the Administrative Council shall act on behalf of the Plenipotentiary Conference within the limits of the powers delegated to it by the latter." According to the General Regulations of the Vienna Constitution, the UPU Executive Council is composed of twenty-seven members (raised to thirty-one by the Tokyo Congress; see Article 102 of the General Regulations). The number of members of the ITU Administrative Council is twenty-nine. In the election of both Councils the principle of equitable geographical distribution of seats is respected.

9. See Alexandrowicz, *supra* note 1, Chapter 1, pp. 284–85.

10. Administrative Conferences are the concern of postal administrations and not of governments and thus are composed of experts and not diplomats. See also Article 56 of the ICAO Convention, which requires technical qualifications from members of the Air Navigation Commission (ANC). But an analysis of conventions shows that special qualifications of a technical nature are not stipulated for representatives of member states to plenary organs.

11. Codding, *supra* note 6, pp. 396–97.

12. The Commission has been renamed Council at the Tokyo Congress (1969).

13. A Committee of Education was also established in Vienna.

14. The chief executive officer and his personnel act not multilaterally but unilaterally, subject to their responsibility to the representative organs.

15. The chief executive officers of ILO developed a pattern of international statesmanship, but this example was not followed by the secretary-general of the League of Nations. With regard to the United Nations, see *The Strategy of World Order* (1966), ed. by Falk and Mendlowitz, Vol. 3, p. 304.

16. ICAO News Release, November, 1970. *See also* 25 ICAO *Bull.*, p. 27, December, 1970. China is represented by the Formosan government; Poland and Czechoslovakia are members of ICAO.

17. The Council is a permanent organ (Article 50). Apart from the quasi-legislative functions it also performs judicial and administrative functions. The Council elects its president for a term of three years. He has international status, and in this respect he is on the same level as the secretary-general and the personnel of ICAO (Article 59) and has the same privileges and immunities (Article 60).

18. As to the definition of chief importance it may be asked whether it depends on the international traffic of a state or also on its internal traffic. Is the business of its airline(s) or the size of its aircraft essential? These may be important factors for fixing a state's budget contributions and for defining chief importance. The expression *not otherwise included* must mean "not otherwise elected." Mankiewicz, "L'Organisation de l'aviation civile internationale," 5 *Ann. Fran. Droit Int'l*, pp. 549–51 (1959).

19. Mankiewicz, "L'Organisation de l'aviation civile internationale," 8 *Ann. Fran. Droit Int'l*, pp. 675–78 (1962).

20. The Council appoints the members and defines the duties of the Air Transport Committee. The members "shall be chosen from among the representations of the members of the Council and . . . shall be responsible to it." The Council cannot interfere in this manner with the Commission, which has a constitutionally guaranteed position (Articles 56–57). See Sheffy, "The Air Navigation Commission of International Civil Aviation Organization," 25 *J. Air L. & Com.*, pp. 281, 428 (1958).

21. The Commission establishes panels of highly specialized experts who carry out the first preparatory work prior to the technical meetings of the divisions. The following divisions can be distinguished: (1) AGA (aerodromes, air routes, ground aids); (2) AIG (accident investigation); (3) AIR (airworthiness, nationality, and registration marks); (4) COM (aeronautical telecommunication, radio aids, air navigation); (5) MAP (aeronautical maps and charts); (6) MET (meteorology); (7) OPS (operations); (8) PEL (personnel licensing); (9) RAC (rules of the air and air traffic control); (10) SAR (search and rescue); (11) AIS (aeronautical information services). While the divisions prepare the draft Annexes, the Commission modifies these drafts only if absolutely necessary.

22. Article 18 (amended).

23. Not in practice.

24. As to the procedure of nomination of the secretary-general, see Mankiewicz, "L'Organisation de l'Aviation Civile Internationale," 13 *Ann. Fran. Droit Int'l*, pp. 482, 485–86 (1967).

25. UPU was able to carry out modifications of the texts through the interval procedure instead of administrative conferences.

26. Subject to minor exceptions.

27. As to the UPU Executive Council, see Article 17 of the Constitution and Article 102 of the General Regulations. As to the ITU Administrative Council, see Article 9 of the convention. It meets only once a year as a rule.

28. Reinsch, *supra* note 6, p. 145.

29. Reinsch, *id.,* p. 139.

30. Labeyrie-Menahem, *Des Institutions Specialisées* (1953), pp. 76–103.

31. Although the procedure of opting out is provided (see the discussion at pp. 49–50, above).

CHAPTER FIVE
ARBITRATION PROCEDURES

1. Disputes between UPU members cannot be referred to the International Court of Justice in contentious proceedings. Neither can UPU directly ask the Court for an Advisory Opinion.

2. For a survey of UPU arbitral cases, see *Code Annoté,* pp. 49–56.

3. The jurisdiction of the International Court of Justice in contentious proceedings is available to the parties to a dispute. Moreover, ITU can directly ask the Court for an Advisory Opinion as can ICAO and IMCO. IMCO did so in 1960.

4. See submission to the Council of the Indo-Pakistan dispute over Indian air transport services between Delhi and Kabul. Alexandrowicz, *World Economic Agencies,* p. 142(n)(1962).

CHAPTER SIX
MIXED PUBLIC AND PRIVATE AGENCIES IN THE FIELD
OF GLOBAL COMMUNICATION

1. See Alexandrowicz, *id.,* p. 152.

2. "The Association may exercise its functions throughout Canada or elsewhere and meetings of the Association may be held at any place other than the Head Office of the Association and either within or without Canada." (Act of Incorporation, p. 9).

3. The number of IATA's members exceeds one hundred airlines carrying 90 per cent of the world's scheduled air transport. But nonscheduled air transport is steadily increasing.

4. Guinchard, "L'International Air Transport Association," 2 *Ann. Fran. Droit Int'l,* pp. 666, 668 (1956). The view has been expressed that the reduction of air fares is due to pressure from the CAB (USA) rather than to IATA policy.

5. The Traffic Advisory Committee, the Technical Committee, the Financial Committee, the Legal Committee, and the Medical Committee.

6. Apart from rates and fares for passengers and cargo, Traffic Conferences are in charge of international traffic matters involving passengers, mail, and cargo, for example, the analysis of operating costs and schedules.

7. Cheng, *The Law of International Air Transport* (1962), pp. 246–51.

8. Traffic Conferences may consist of voting and nonvoting members. Each active member of IATA who operates a scheduled commercial international air service between a single point within the area of one Traffic Conference and one or more points in another Traffic Conference area is qualified for voting membership in both such Traffic Conferences and must become a voting member in one of these conferences.

9. A government's concern is determined by the nationality (place of incorporation) of an airline.

10. As to the difference of views between the United States and European carriers on the date of effectiveness of rate agreements, see Cheng, *supra* note 7, pp. 246–51.

11. In that case other carriers would be prevented from entering into agreements. Cheng, *id.*, pp. 246–51.

12. P. 105.

13. See Traffic Conferences in Cannes (1968), Dallas, Nassau, Los Angeles, Caracas (1969). A conference was held in Honolulu in September, 1970.

14. Resolution IV of the Fifth General Meeting provides that a Commission is authorized to impose on a member of a Traffic Conference the following penalties for breach of conference obligations: (1) notification to all members of the findings of the Commission; (2) reprimand; (3) a fine for breach of a conference resolution not in excess of U.S. $25,000; (4) expulsion from IATA.

15. Bebchick, "The International Air Transport Association and the Civil Aeronautics Board," 25 *J. Air L. & Com.*, p. 8 (1958).

16. As to the role of private agencies in UPU and ITU, see Reinsch, *Public International Unions* (1911), p. 21. In 1868 ITU admitted private agencies to participation in the work of the organization.

17. The East India companies are earlier examples of private agencies which were active in the field of global communication. See Alexandrowicz, *An Introduction to the History of the Law of Nations in the East Indies, 16th, 17th, and 18th Centuries* (1967).

18. The assimilation of IATA to public international agencies also has its restrictive effects. Thus, according to an amendment of the Articles of Association of IATA (Section 21, b), expulsion of IATA members from ICAO results, under certain conditions, in their expulsion from IATA. See *IATA Bulletin*, 1966.

19. See Legislation Note, "The Communications Satellite Act of 1962," 76 *Harv. L. Rev.* 388–400 (1962–1963).

20. Moulton, "Commercial Space Communications," in *Space and Society* (H. Taubenfeld ed. 1964), p. 73; Colino, "INTELSAT: Doing Business in Outer Space," 6 *Colum. J. Transnat'l L.* 17 (1967).

21. If FCC should fail to exercise its powers consistently with the purposes of the act, the president could control satellite development.

22. According to S.102(c) of the act, the activities of the Corporation and of the persons or companies participating in its ownership must be consistent with federal antitrust laws. The FCC has a duty to promote competition and to assure nondiscriminatory access to the system.

23. It seems that this act would not control the international powers and functions of the Corporation, particularly those exercised within the framework of INTELSAT.

24. Three of the latter would be controlled by AT&T, the most important carrier. AT&T has 29 per cent of shares of COMSAT, ITT has 10.5 per cent, GTE, 3.5 per cent, and RCA, 2.5 per cent. The four carriers jointly have 45.5 per cent of the shares.

25. See *Report of the Postmaster General, Cmnd* No. 2436 (1964). The Corporation is authorized to "furnish for hire, channels of communication to the United States common carriers and to other authorised entities, foreign and domestic; and to own and operate satellite terminal stations."

26. *Id.*

27. *Id.*

28. See statement by one of the under-secretaries before the Senate Aeronautical and Space Sciences Committee on the February 28, 1962, in which he called ITU a "regulatory" body and thus unfit to be an operating agency, Moulton, *supra* note 20, p. 84.

29. See *Report of the Postmaster General, supra* note 25.

30. In a criticism of the Washington twin agreement before the British House of Commons Estimates Committee, it was emphasized that the place of COMSAT as manager should be handed over to a truly international organ and that the "majority" quota of the United States (50.6 per cent) should be abandoned and a more equitable distribution of votes adopted. *Financial Times,* London, February 5, 1968.

31. The difference has more a legal than an economic character. Even government entities will endeavor to be profit making while private entities are in certain respects under public supervision. However, the difference was significant enough to have called for two agreements in the international sphere.

32. The OTC was established in 1946 by Act of Parliament. It is a body corporate, functioning under the direction of the PMG. OTC is responsible for the fulfillment of Australia's obligations under the Commonwealth Telegraph Agreement which established a partnership between the countries of the Commonwealth in telecommunication services. This means Commonwealth cooperation within the wider framework of ITU.

33. These examples are drawn from the list of founder members.

34. Article II of the principal agreement states that "each party either shall sign or shall designate a communication entity, public or private, to sign the special agreement. . . . Relations between any such designated entity and the party which has designated it shall be governed by the applicable domestic law." Does it mean that the designated entity does not act as the delegate of a sovereign? If not, the Special Agreement is not a treaty in the strict sense of the word. But such a conclusion is not acceptable in practice.

35. If the other entity is a private agency, the state on whose territory the agency is established would be responsible for its actions within the framework of ITU (see Article 21 of the ITU Convention).

36. Batailler, "Les accords relatifs à l'exploitation commerciale des satellites de télécommunications." 11 *Ann. Fran. Droit Int'l,* p. 145 (1965).

37. As to the original United States' proposals, see Colino, *supra* note 20, p. 40.

38. Batailler, *supra* note 36.

39. According to Article III of the principal agreement "the space segment (is) owned in undivided shares by the signatories to the Special Agreement in proportion to their respective contributions to the costs of the design, development, construction, and establishment of the space segment." This contribution is, according to Article 3 of the Special Agreement, equal to the quota which determines the voting rights—thus the close interrelationship between financial and technical power and the control of the system.

40. The initial quotas of the European countries were jointly 30.5 per cent.

41. See Article XII(c) of the principal agreement.

42. Alexandrowicz, *supra* note 1, ch. I, Introduction.

43. Most important decisions in INTELSAT have been taken unanimously or by very substantial majorities. See the comments of J. A. Johnson, vice-president of COMSAT, [1967] *Proc. Am. Soc. Int'l L.,* p. 43; Colino, *supra* note 20, p. 46.

44. Whenever the objective is the achievement of basic global coverage in the latter part of 1969. See Article I, a, ii.

45. The same applies to decisions mentioned in Article V(a) relating to certain budgetary and technical questions.

46. The number of contracting parties is gradually rising (at present seventy-five). See Colino, *supra* note 20, p. 40; on January 1, 1970, seventy-one states were parties.

47. In the light of the provisions of the principal agreement it cannot fall below 50 per cent (50.63). As to criticism of the distribution of voting power, see Johnson, "International Co-operation in Satellite Communications Systems," [1967] *Proc. Am. Soc. Int'l L.,* pp. 24, 25–26; Woetzel, "International Co-operation in Telecommunication for Educational and Cultural Purposes," *id.,* pp. 29, 32–36; and comments at *id.,* pp. 43, 43–46, 47–48.

48. Batailler, *supra* note 36.

49. See Simsarion, "Interim Arrangements for a Global Commercial Communications Satellite System," 59 *Am. J. Int'l L.*, p. 344 (1965).

50. The chance of accession of the Soviet Union is remote. But the latter has concluded an agreement with France, and NASA has made arrangements with the Soviet Academy of Sciences in respect of Echo 2 and other experiments.

51. Batailler, *supra* note 36. A majority of member countries of INTELSAT have quotas of less than one per cent at present. In fact, the Committee is composed of seventeen members representing forty of the fifty-six members. This means that a certain number of countries is chronically unrepresented. See Johnson, *supra* note 47, pp. 25–26.

52. Article X of the principal agreement states that "when proposals or tenders are determined to be comparable in terms of quality, c.i.f. price and timely performance, the Committee and the Corporation as manager shall also seek to ensure that contracts are so distributed that equipment is designed, developed, and procured in the States whose Governments are Parties to this agreement in approximate proportion to the respective quotas of their corresponding signatories in the Special Agreement. . . ." According to Article 10 of the Special Agreement, the approval of the Committee is required before contracts are placed by the Corporation or by any other signatory (pursuant to authorization by the Committee). But the contracts are actually selected by the Corporation, and all contracts are in the name of the Corporation and are executed and administered by it as manager.

53. Further details relating to the utilization of the space segment can be found in Article VII of the principal agreement, which requires approval of the Committee for such utilization and in Articles 7 and 8 of the Special Agreement, which deal with multiple access to satellites, applications of earth stations for permission to utilize the space segment and the duties of the applicant such as equitable and nondiscriminatory access of all signatories to utilizing earth stations. Three phases of satellite development are anticipated: (1) A global system of low-powered satellites serving high-powered ground stations linked with conventional distribution networks. This system would provide telephone and telegraph services of the same quality as present services, and there would also be facilities for relay of sound and visual broadcasting; (2) A system of high-powered satellites and lower-powered ground stations. This would furnish direct communication between cities and perhaps direct broadcasts to homes; (3) A comprehensive system of manned satellites linking cities, countries, and continents directly.

54. See Batailler, *supra* note 36, who draws our attention to the *dédoublement fonctionnel* involved in this situation.

55. Woetzel, *supra* note 47. See also the comments by Woetzel, [1967] *Proc. Am. Soc. Int'l L.*, pp. 43, 46; and Johnson, *id.* pp. 43, 45–46.

56. Report of the I.L.A. (1967), pp. 203–15.

57. The Washington agreements concentrate on the use of satellites for services of public correspondence, and they do not deal with the organization of Radio

and TV transmissions by satellites designated for direct reception by the public (without the use of receiving ground stations).

58. Comments of Lee Marks, [1967] *Proc. Am. Soc. Int'l L.,* p. 44. Attention may also be drawn to Article 13, which states as follows: "Neither the Corporation as signatory or manager, nor any other signatory as such shall be liable to any other signatory for loss or damage sustained by reason of a failure or break down of a satellite at or after launching or a failure or break down of any other portion of the space segment." The article refers to the absence of liability "to any other signatory," not to other entities such as nonsignatories or to third persons.

59. Friedmann, "The Changing Dimensions of International Law," 62 *Colum. L. Rev.,* pp. 1147, 1160 (1962). The author examines the characteristic features of the multinational company, a form of organization which is partly a public international agency and partly a private corporation operating in the international field. An example is Eurofima, a European railway agency established in 1955. See also Eurochemic.

60. The question may arise whether states can submit their disputes in connection with the Special Agreement to the International Court of Justice. Article 14 refers only to disputes arising in connection with the Special Agreement which is not an interstate agreement. But the close connection between the two agreements would perhaps justify the assumption of jurisdiction by the Court.

61. Johnson, *supra* note 47, p. 26.

62. The Supplementary INTELSAT Agreement declares the decision of the arbitral tribunal to be binding on all parties to the dispute. Where the Committee is a party, a decision of the tribunal that a particular action of the Committee is null and void is binding on all signatories.

63. Synchronous satellites are in orbit 22,000 miles above the earth at the equator. They travel as fast as the earth rotates on its axis. As the orbit is synchronized with the earth's rotation, the satellite appears to be stationary relative to a particular spot on earth.

64. Intelsat I has a capacity of 240 circuits and an estimated lifetime of eighteen months or more; Intelsat II will provide 360 circuits and a three-year lifetime; Intelsat III is expected to have 1,200 circuits and a five-year lifetime. See Colino, *supra* note 20, p. 47.

65. The Intersessional Working Group of INTELSAT recommended that, at the future Plenipotentiary Conference of INTELSAT (to be held in May, 1971), the interim Washington Agreements should be revised in order to adopt a more equitable distribution of votes (quotas) among member countries and to substitute a truly international managing body in place of COMSAT. See the *Times,* February 12, 1971, p. 20.

66. [1967] *Proc. Am. Soc. Int'l L.,* pp. 46–47.

67. *Id.,* p. 47.

68. For instance, the convention relating to the law of salvage and collision at sea (1910) and the original Convention on Safety at Sea, which was concluded after the Titanic disaster in 1912.

69. [1960] *I.C.J. Reports* 150.

CHAPTER SEVEN

THE NATIONALITY OF VEHICLES OF GLOBAL COMMUNICATION
AND THE TECHNIQUE OF REGISTRATION

1. Mankiewicz, "Les aéronefs internationaux," 8 *Ann. Fran. Droit Int'l*, p. 685. (1962).

2. McNair, *The Law of the Air* (1954), p. 260.

3. As to the fiction of territoriality, see Colombos, *International Law of the Sea* (1967), pp. 285–88. The author disagrees with the relevant conclusions reached by the P.C.I.J. in the *Lotus* case.

4. The term pseudo-territory is not synonymous with fictional territory. Colombos, *id.*, pp. 285–88.

5. The principle of autonomy of conferring nationality on a merchant ship has been emphasized in Lauritzen v. Larsen, 345, U.S. 571 (1953). In some states a proportion only of owners must be nationals of a particular state, e.g., Belgium, Greece, and Italy. Colombos, *supra* note 3, p. 290.

6. Colombos, *supra* note 3, p. 290. Some states require that officers and part of the crew should be nationals of the registering state.

7. See Boczek, *Flags of Convenience* (1962). As to the position of Panlibhon ships in United States' harbors, see Benz v. Comp. Navierra Hidalgo, 353 U.S. 138 (1957), in which the Supreme Court held that the Labor Management Relations Act (Taft-Hartley Act) of 1947 did not apply to a dispute concerning damages which resulted from picketing of a ship registered in Liberia, but owned by a Panamanian Corporation. Thus the Court gave expression to the American practice that the law of the flag governs the internal regime of a foreign ship regardless of ownership. The National Labor Relations Board (NLRB) held in West India Fruit and Steamship Company, 130 N.L.R.B. 343 (1961), that the Labor Management Relations Act applied to American ships flying foreign flags, manned by nonresident aliens and operating from United States' ports. The NLRB expressed the view that the transfer of vessels to Panlibhon flags is not supported by the policy of Congress. But see McCulloch v. Sociedad Nacional de Marinieros de Honduras, 372 U.S. 10 (1963).

8. The word "shipowning" has nothing to do with ownership but indicates the amount of registered tonnage.

9. The text of Article 28 has been amended. See IMCO Basic Documents, March, 1968, p. 14.

10. Constitution of the Maritime Safety Committee of the Inter-Governmental Maritime Consultative Organization, Advisory Opinion of June 8, 1960, *I. C. J. Reports* 1960, p. 150; see Simmonds, "The Constitution of the Maritime Safety

Committee of IMCO," 12 *Int'l & Comp. L. Q.*, p. 56 (1963); Johnson, "IMCO: The First Four Years (1959–1962)," 12 *Int'l & Comp. L. Q.*, p. 31 (1963).

11. English municipal law adopted the concept of the genuine link in shipping and civil aviation. See Merchant Shipping Act (1894), and Air Navigation Order (1960).

12. Registration, it was alleged, is not the same thing as beneficial ownership of tonnage.

13. See Simmonds, *supra* note 10.

14. *Id.*

15. Simmonds, *id.* The author also emphasizes the difficulties connected with the frequent change in registered tonnage figures. On the other hand McDougal and Burke (*The Public Order of the Oceans* (1962), p. 1140) expressed the view that the states of the world should reject the segment of Article 5 [Geneva Convention on the High Seas] which expresses the requirement of genuine link."

16. As to the origin of the clause, see Goedhuis, "Problems of Public International Air Law," [1957] 2 *Recueil des Cours* 205, and Wassenbergh, *supra* Chapter I, note 26, p. 158.

17. Thus a foreign airline may employ leased or chartered aircraft. A survey of bilateral air transport agreements carried out by ICAO (circular 63-AT/6) shows certain variations in the formulation of this clause in various agreements. Sometimes the clause allows revocation, or withholding, of rights of substantial ownership and effective control if not vested "in nationals of either contracting party" or "in the nationals of the other contracting party." The Chicago wording is "nationality of a party to this agreement." The clause appears not only in bilateral agreements but also in the Two Freedom and the Five Freedom Agreements. See Cheng, *The Law of International Air Transport* (1960), p. 375.

18. Provided the airline fulfills all other conditions.

19. Under the Paris Convention of 1919 (Article 7) no aircraft could be entered on a register of a contracting state "unless it belongs wholly to nationals of such State." Thus registration of convenience was ruled out. The further text of Article 7 referred to the registration of companies as owners of aircraft prescribing a number of conditions such as the nationality of the company, of its chairman, of the majority of directors, and so on. This clause was amended in 1929 and the autonomy of the contracting states, in respect to registration of aircraft, was restored.

20. Whatever the situation may be in international law, municipal law varies from country to country, and in some countries registration of aircraft as well as ships does not depend on the nationality of the owner, while in other countries nationality is a condition of registration. See, for instance, the situation in the United Kingdom under the Air Navigation Order (1960) and under the Merchant Shipping Act (1894). While aircraft and ships would be registered under the condition that the owner is a British subject (or British-protected person), foreign controlled companies may under certain conditions become the registered owners of British aircraft or ships. McNair, *supra* note 2, p. 306.

21. Report of the Fifty-second Conference of the International Law Association in 1966, published in 1967, p. 260. See Mankiewicz in 13 *Ann. Fran. Droit Int'l*, pp. 482, 487–501 (1967), who considers the possible amendment of the ICAO Convention (Articles 18,77). See also Article 18 of the Tokyo Convention of 1963.

22. The ICAO Council adopted in 1967 a Resolution on Nationality and Registration of Aircraft operated by International Operating Agencies. It stated that "in the case of aircraft which are jointly registered or internationally registered and in respect of which the basic criteria which have been established by the Council are fulfilled, the rights and obligations under the (ICAO) Convention would be applicable as in the case of nationally registered aircraft of a Contracting State." Such aircraft "shall, for the purposes of the Convention, be deemed to have the nationality of each of the States constituting the international operating agency." Dec. 8/22-C/976, 20/2/68.

23. Among the private international law conventions the most significant is the Warsaw Convention of 1929, which has been amended by the Hague Protocol of 1955. This convention establishes uniform rules governing the rights and duties of international air carriers and passengers (consignors, consignees of goods). It applies to international carriage by air of persons, luggage, and goods by reward and also to gratuitous carriage by air if performed by a transport enterprise. In 1964 the Guadalajara Convention was concluded. It refers to the case of international carriage by air performed by a person (the actual carrier) who is not a party to the agreement for carriage (concluded by the contracting carrier). According to the Convention both carriers are subject to the rules of the Warsaw Convention, amended or not amended. In 1965 the United States gave notice of denunciation of the Warsaw Convention. In 1966 it withdrew the notice after agreement with a number of airlines was reached at Montreal, which made these airlines absolutely liable up to $75,000 per passenger. The agreement is only provisional and a new amendment of the convention will be required (See *IATA Bulletin* (1966) and Mankiewicz *supra* note 21, pp. 507–24. The ICAO-sponsored Conventions of the postwar period remained under-ratified (see Geneva, Rome, and Tokyo Conventions). The Geneva Convention on the International Recognition of Rights in Aircraft of 1948 is of the "recognition" type as distinguished from the "unification" type. A convention on damage caused by foreign aircraft to third parties on the surface was concluded in Rome in 1952 (see *ICAO Bulletin*, Vol. XX, No. 6 (1965)). The Legal Committee of ICAO considered also the following matters: liability for damage to aircraft caused by space vehicles; carrier's liability for carriage of mail; the Vienna Convention on civil liability for nuclear damage; and the proposals for a convention on aerial collisions (*IATA Bulletin*, No. 11/1 (1964)). The ICAO Council convened an Extraordinary Meeting of the Assembly (June, 1970) to consider a convention relating the illicit seizure of aircraft. *ICAO Bulletin*, May–June, 1970.

24. In this respect the municipal laws of states are not uniform. A majority of states applies the territorial principle of jurisdiction subject to the concurrent (personal) jurisdiction in certain cases. Colombos, *supra* note 3, p. 309.

25. Also in case the assistance of local authorities has been requested by the captain of the ship or if it is necessary for the supervision of illicit traffic in narcotic drugs.

26. See the case of the "Amiral Hamelin" (*Brit. Y. B. Int'l L.,* 1920–21, p. 82); decisions of the French Conseil d'Etat in "the Sally" and "the Newton," *Bulletin des lois* (1806), No. 126, p. 602; the American decisions in the Wildenhus' Case, 120 U.S. 1, 12 (1887); United States v. Flores, 289 U.S. 137, 158 (1933); Lauritzen v. Larsen, 345 U.S. 571 (1953); West India Fruit & Steamship Co. 130 N.L.R.B. 343 (1961); McCulloch v. Sociedad Nacional de Marineros de Honduras, 372 U.S. 10 (1963). See Colombos, *supra* note 3, p. 326. "All matters of discipline and all things done on board" which do not involve the peace and tranquility of the port in which the ship found itself on its international route should be left to the jurisdiction of the flag state. In principle the same rules apply in ports as in territorial waters but subject to modifications as the interests of the coastal state are more directly affected in ports. Colombos, *supra* note 3, p. 319. As to the differences between the regime in the territorial sea and the regime in internal waters, see "Institute of International Law," *Annuaire de l'Institut de droit international,* Vol. II, p. 167 *et. seq.*

27. Several countries (e.g., Spain) apply their municipal law (civil and criminal) on board aircraft when the latter are abroad. See Mankiewicz, "Aéronefs Internationaux," 8 *Ann. Fran. Droit Int'l,* pp. 685, 707–708 (1962). The law of registration may often be the proper law of contract of carriage according to principles of private international law. McNair, *supra* note 2, p. 270.

28. [1956] 2 Q.B. 272.

29. [1961] 2 All E.R. 932.

30. The indictment relied on Section 2 of the Larceny Act (1916). The aircraft was over the high seas at the time of commission of the offense.

31. The question may arise whether the above law would also apply to BOAC aircraft registered outside England.

32. The judge in the first case adopted the rule of nonextension of English law to British aircraft subject to exceptions, namely, universal offenses. In the second case the judge reversed the order of rule and exception and considered English law applicable on board British aircraft subject to exceptions in case of offenses of domestic application. See also Cox v. Army Council, [1963] A.C.48, in which one of the judges cast doubt on the classification of offenses into domestic and other offenses.

33. See also United States v. Cordova, 89 F.Supp. 298 (E.D.N.Y. 1950). In this case it was held that a statute relating to crimes committed on ships on the high seas did not apply to aircraft. See subsequent amendment of S.7 of Title 18 of the U.S. Code. McNair, *supra* note 2, p. 272.

34. Lopez Gutierrez, "Should the Tokyo Convention of 1963 be Ratified?" 31 *J. Air L. & Com.* 1, (1965). The Tokyo Convention Act of 1967 (Commencement) Order 1968 has brought into force, on April 1, 1968, the Tokyo Convention Act of

1967 with the exception of S.2. The act enabled the United Kingdom to ratify the convention.

35. *Id.*

36. See also Article 12 of the Chicago Convention, which states *inter alia* that "over the high seas the rules [of the air] in force shall be those established under this convention." Thus the international standards relating to the rules of the air are in this case binding on the contracting parties. According to the further text of the article the contracting states undertake to adopt measures to ensure that every aircraft flying within its territory and every aircraft carrying its nationality mark [wherever it be] shall comply with the regulations relating to flight and maneuver of aircraft there in force. Finally, "each contracting State undertakes [under Article 12] to ensure the prosecution of all persons violating the regulations applicable." Thus each contracting state will prosecute persons violating: (1) its own regulations; (2) regulations in force in other contracting states; and (3) regulations in force over the high seas and possibly in any area beyond national sovereignty.

37. Or any other state at 1–4.

38. Gutierrez, *supra* note 34. As to unlawful seizure of aircraft, see Article 11 of the Tokyo Convention and the ICAO Assembly Meeting of 1970. As to action taken by the UN General Assembly and ICAO, see van Panhuys, "Aircraft Hijacking and International Law," 9 *Colum. J. Transnat'l L.* 1 (1970). The author concludes that "a general duty of states to cooperate in the suppression of air piracy" may be assumed to exist as an unwritten rule of international law. Thus the principles underlying sea piracy can be applied *per analogiam.* The ideal solution would be to adopt a treaty based on the Grotian formula "aut punire aut dedere" (either punish or extradite). As to the plea of political crime the author thinks that in most cases it is not justifiable.

39. British Parliament passed the Tokyo Convention Act of 1967 (see *Current Law Statutes,* 1967, Part 5, Chapter 52). Section 1 of the act states that "any act or omission taking place on board a British controlled aircraft while in flight elsewhere than in or over the United Kingdom which, if taking place in [the UK] would constitute an offence under the law in force [in the UK] shall constitute that offence." This section does away with the juridical classification of offenses into universal offenses and offenses of domestic application. As to jurisdiction, the Section reproduces S.62(1) of the Civil Aviation Act of 1949, which "is hereby repealed." Section 2 contains provisions relating to extradition, section 3 relates to the powers of the aircraft commander, and section 4 relates to piracy. The Schedule to the Act contains the provisions of Articles 15 to 17 of the Geneva Convention on the High Seas relating to piracy in connection with ship and aircraft.

40. Report of the Fifty-second Conference of the International Law Association in 1966 (published in 1967, p. 215). Registration of spacecraft can, according to UN resolutions, be national or international. But the establishment of a definite legal regime covering all branches of law would require municipal registration in any event. See G. Lafferranderie, "Le Statut Juridique du Satellite de Télécom-

munication," in *Les Télécommunications par Satellites, aspects juridiques,* ed. by Centre National de la Recherche Scientifique (CNRS).

41. See Chapter I, note 75 *et. seq.*

42. While there would be no conflict between the law of nationality of the spacecraft and any foreign territorial law, there might be conflicts between the former and other laws such as the law of the nationality of the offender or the victim of the offense.

43. There is no need to dwell on speculations relating to legal systems prevailing anywhere beyond the earth.

CHAPTER EIGHT

LEGAL FACTORS SUPPORTING THE GLOBALITY OF AGENCIES OF INTERNATIONAL COMMUNICATION

1. Alexandrowicz, *World Economic Agencies,* p. 4 (1962).

2. The UPU Constitution was amended in Tokyo (1969) by an additional protocol which came into force on July 1, 1970. Member states which did not sign this protocol can adhere to it at any time. Member states which are parties to Acts of the Union amended by the Tokyo Congress but which have not signed them are under duty to adhere to them as soon as possible. See Article VII of the protocol.

3. Mankiewicz, "L'Organisation de l'Aviation Civile International," 11 *Ann. Fran. Droit Int'l,* pp. 630–35 (1965). Moreover, Article 93 bis has been added to the ICAO Convention, making membership of certain states dependent on action by the United Nations General Assembly which may expel or suspend states (UN members) or make recommendations detrimental to such states.

4. See also the sanctions provided in Article 41 of the United Nations Charter according to which the Security Council may call upon its members to apply certain measures against a state. These measures may include complete or partial interruption of means of communication (sea, air, postal, telegraph, radio, and so on).

5. The Executive and Liaison Commission (UPU) admitted, in 1950, the delegates of the Peking government as "the only qualified representatives of China." This decision was later reversed. The Peking delegates were never admitted by ITU. See Codding, *International Telecommunication Union* (1952), pp. 417–19.

6. The adoption of a new convention resulted in the abrogation of the previous convention and left the nonratifying country in a legal vacuum as far as international postal services were concerned. See also Article 18 of the Montreux Convention according to which instruments of ratification shall be deposited with the secretary-general of ITU in "as short a time as possible." During the period of two years after entry into force of the convention, a signatory enjoys membership rights even in the absence of ratification. After two years a signatory loses the right to vote.

7. *Code Annoté*, p. 43.

8. A view which disregards the constitutional character of the convention. See Codding, *supra* note 5, pp. 230–31.

9. But see the efforts of the Afro-Asian group to expel South Africa (and Portugal) from the organizations.

10. [1949] *I.C.J. Reports* 174.

CHAPTER NINE

SUMMARY AND CONCLUSIONS

1. This matter is dealt with in detail in the study of Professor J. Andrassy, *International Law and the Resources of the Sea* (1970).

2. Tending to emphasize its functional quality.

3. Generally speaking, the sanctions of expulsion and suspension of privileges of membership are not available in the Constitutions of the agencies of global communication. But see Article 11, IMCO, and Article 93 bis, ICAO (expulsion from the organization in case of expulsion from the United Nations), and Article 42, IMCO, and Article 62, ICAO (suspension of voting rights in case of failure of discharging the financial obligations to the organization).

4. It is proposed to convert the Consortium into a permanent organization. According to the proposals (Report of Intersessional Working Group, December 1970), two agreements would be concluded—an intergovernmental agreement and an operating agreement, signed by states and designated Telecommunication entities. The organization would have four organs: the Assembly of Contracting Parties, which is a plenary organ in which each party has one vote (it is concerned with political and external affairs); the Plenary Meeting of Signatories, each having one vote, concerned with internal affairs of the organization; the Board of Governors, which retains the system of weighted voting (no representative may have more than 40 per cent of the total voting power); and the Executive Organ, headed by the director-general. See Ch. VI, note 65, *supra*.

5. Friedmann, *The Changing Structure of International Law* (1964), pp. 88–95. As shown above, some of the standards have a self-mandatory quality that is sometimes inherent in the subject matter of regulation, particularly in the field of radiocommunication.

INDEX